CW00484972

AFPC

PRACTICE & REVISION KIT

Paper G60

Pensions

- This Practice & Revision Kit contains the equivalent of five examinations, providing candidates with the essential opportunity of question practice and so helping ensure exam success.

- Key Fact Tests highlight the required knowledge for this exam and allow candidates to identify weaknesses.

- Two mock exams ensure your final preparation is focused on the task in hand – success.

UPDATES ARE AVAILABLE ON OUR WEBSITE AT:

www.bpp.com/fpc

BPP Publishing
July 2001

First edition February 2000
Third edition July 2001

ISBN 0 7517 9820 7 (previous edition 0 7517 9811 8)

British Library Cataloguing-in-Publication Data
A catalogue record for this book
is available from the British Library

Published by

BPP Publishing Limited
Aldine House, Aldine Place
London W12 8AW

www.bpp.com

Printed by DA COSTA PRINT
1 Mildmay Avenue
London N1 4RS
Telephone 0207 354 6200

All our rights reserved. No part of this publication may be reproduced, stored in a retrieval system or transmitted, in any form or by any means, electronic, mechanical, photocopying, recording or otherwise, without the prior written permission of BPP Publishing Limited.

We are grateful to the Chartered Insurance Institute for permission to reproduce in this Kit references to the syllabus of which the Institute holds the copyright.

©
BPP Publishing Limited
2001

CONTENTS

BPP PUBLISHING

Introduction

You're taking professional exams. You're under time pressure to get your exam revision done. And trying to fit in study as well as a social life around your job is difficult. Could you make better use of your time? Are you sure that your revision is really relevant to the exam you will be facing?

If you use BPP revision material you can be sure that the time you spend revising and practising questions is time well spent. Our **Practice & Revision Kits** are clear, concise and effective and are focused exclusively on what you, the candidate, can expect to encounter in your exam.

- We offer **guidance on revision, question practice and exam technique** gleaned from years of successfully helping students to pass their AFPC exams.

- We highlight the format of the exam that you will face and ensure that all of the **exam standard questions in the Kit** reflect that format.

- We ensure that **the questions are comprehensive** so that you can cover all areas of the syllabus if you have time.

REVISION GUIDE

How to revise

This is a very important time as you approach the exam. You must remember three things.

> **Use time sensibly**
> **Set realistic goals**
> **Believe in yourself**

Use time sensibly

1   **How much study time do you have?** Remember that you must EAT, SLEEP, and of course, RELAX.

2   **How will you split that available time between each subject?** What are your weaker subjects? They need more time.

3   **What is your learning style?** AM/PM? Little and often/long sessions? Evenings/ weekends?

4   **Are you taking regular breaks?** Most people absorb more if they do not attempt to study for long uninterrupted periods of time. A five minute break every hour (to make coffee, watch the news headlines) can make all the difference.

5   **Do you have quality study time?** Unplug the phone. Let everybody know that you're studying and shouldn't be disturbed.

Set realistic goals

1   Have you set a **clearly defined objective** for each study period?

2   Is the objective **achievable**?

3   Will you **stick to your plan**? Will you make up for any **lost time**?

4   Are you **rewarding yourself** for your hard work?

5   Are you leading a **healthy lifestyle**?

Believe in yourself

Are you cultivating the right attitude of mind? There is absolutely no reason why you should not pass this exam if you adopt the correct approach

- **Be confident** - you've passed exams before, you can pass them again
- **Be calm** - plenty of adrenaline but no panicking
- **Be focused** - commit yourself to passing the exam

(v)

Exam technique

Passing professional examinations is half about having the knowledge, and half about doing yourself full justice in the examination. You must have the right technique.

> ### The day of the exam

1   Set at least one **alarm** (or get an alarm call) for a morning exam

2   Have **something to eat** but beware of eating too much; you may feel sleepy if your system is digesting a large meal

3   Allow plenty of **time to get to the exam hall**; have your route worked out in advance and listen to news bulletins to check for potential travel problems

4   **Don't forget** pens, pencils, rulers, erasers

5   Put **new batteries** into your calculator and take a spare set (or a spare calculator)

6   **Avoid discussion** about the exam with other candidates outside the exam hall

> ### Technique in the exam hall

The aim of the Advanced Financial Planning Certificate is to demonstrate that the holder is able to provide a standard of advice which exceeds that normally expected from an FPC level adviser.

The G60 *Pensions* syllabus is certainly set at a much higher standard than the FPC and may be quite a shock to those of you who are taking this paper as a stand-alone qualification, without attempting any other AFPC subjects. The jump in the standard required to pass the exam means that you must be prepared for the different style of questions asked. Combining examination technique with your technical knowledge it is possible to pass this qualification first time!

Firstly you should ensure that you are in possession of a copy of the G60 current syllabus. A copy is contained within the BPP Study Text for this subject. If you don't have a copy you can obtain one directly from the Chartered Insurance Institute or by visiting their website at www.cii.co.uk.

The exam is split into three sections. Section A is a section which consists of a number of short answer questions. These questions tend to span the whole syllabus. This section will account for 45 marks or 22.5% of the total marks available.

Section B is a long case study, which tends to concentrate on pensions transfers. This is the most involved question on the paper and passing this question will be essential to passing the paper as a whole. The question is a compulsory, as is section A. Section B accounts for 75 marks or 37.5% of the exam as a whole.

Section C allows the candidate to choose two questions to answer from three provided. Therefore it is very important that the right two questions are chosen. You must read all three *fully* before deciding which two you are going to choose. It is no use starting a question because you can answer the first part of it, just to realise later on that you are unable to complete the rest of it. This would be a waste of time. This exam is very time pressured and therefore you will have limited you chances of passing the exam by making such a mistake. Section C accounts for 80 marks or 40% of the exam overall.

The pass mark for the exam is thought to be around 55% or 110 marks, although it will be varied slightly from paper to paper to ensure that the standard of candidates passing the exam remains consistent. It is usual for 35% to 45% of the exam to be centred on pensions transfers.

(vi)

Time management

Time management in this exam is vital to ensure that you are able to pass. The time available to complete the exam is 3 hours. There are 200 marks in total available in the exam therefore you need to allocate 54 seconds to acquiring each mark.

The better prepared you are the quicker you will be able to get your ideas down on paper. Time can be acquired in the first section as the answers required are not as involved as those required in both Section B and C.

Each sub-section of the exam is allocated a total of marks available and you should spend an appropriate amount of time in accordance with the marks that are available for that section.

For example, if a sub-section of a question is given 12 marks you know that you will have approximately 10 minutes to answer this section. If you spend four minutes it is a good guide that you have not answered the question in the depth required by the examiner and, equally, if you have spent 25 minutes you will have answered in too much detail.

Ideally you should allocate some time at the end of the exam to read through your answers and correct any obvious mistakes that you have made.

You must be ruthless with your time. Once you have exceeded the time allocated to the question you must leave some space (so you can come back later if you have a few spare moments) and move on to the next question. The reason being that it is easier to acquire marks more easily at the start of a question rather than at the end of the question. This is the 'law of diminishing returns'.

Examination technique

A good idea is to try and obtain at least the examiners report for the most recent sitting. The reason being that it will highlight candidates failings in that exam. It could also have hints as to the examiners thinking for the next session. Normally the CII will send a copy automatically to candidates entered for the exam but not until just before the exam.

Common failings of candidates in this paper

- Not reading the question properly and therefore wasting time writing about issues not requested in the question or a question that has not been set!

- Often candidates do not give all of the steps in a calculation. You need to be aware that there are marks awarded for each step. This is critical. Even if you get the final answer wrong, you will get marks for the correct approach.

- If you are asked to make a recommendation this is all the examiner requires it is not required (unless specifically asked for) to go on and explain the pros and cons of each option.

- When the candidate is asked to list, this is all the examiner wants. There is no need to provide any explanation of the items contained in the list.

- Where a candidate does not have the technical ability to answer the question they tend to 'waffle'. No marks are awarded to 'waffle' it would be better to spend the time elsewhere improving other answers.

- Many candidates do not use the information that is supplied in the tax tables and therefore get calculations wrong. Make sure that you are familiar with what is in the tax tables.

In the exam:

- You should consider how your time is best spent.

- Skimming through the questions before you get started is a good idea because it helps to settle your nerves, it allows you to plan which questions you are going to attempt in Section

C, it will allow you to trigger recall of your notes and also decide to answer your best questions first.

- You should not leave the exam room if you finish within three hours. Try and improve the answers you have given. Read through the material and correct for obvious mistakes.

- There are no 'golden areas' in this exam, ie you only have to get an overall pass mark, it is not possible to get a sectional fail.

- You should use bullet points to answer the questions set. A bullet point is a grammatically correct sentence which simply conveys the answer required. There is no need to repeat the question, the examiner knows what this is, so don't waste time copying it out or including it in the introduction to your answer.

- When asked to give advantages and disadvantages or compare and contrast items it is a good idea to draw up a table and show the items placed at the side of each other. This will help the examiner mark your answer. It is often easier if you are using a table to present it in landscape format rather than the portrait approach invited by the answer book.

- As a general rule of thumb give one bullet point for each mark that is available.

Skills required

The skills tested in the examination

- Recall of facts and figures

- Application of knowledge

- Analysis of complex situations

- Advanced application of knowledge to develop solutions to the situations possible

- Judgement to determine the most appropriate solutions for the situations

Practising questions

Answering questions, after reading a section of the notes, is the most effective way of studying. We only remember about 20% of what we read alone. Comprehension and retention of information rapidly increases if we actively make notes (especially in 'mind map' format) and also answer questions.

The question practice section is split into five areas. There are a number of questions designed to test your knowledge of the syllabus as a whole: the Key Fact Tests. These short questions are rather like section A questions but are designed to ensure that you have picked up the main points from the Study Text. Compare your answers to those provided and highlight in different coloured ink the points that you did not get. It may be the case that you have got an answer that is not shown in the model provided. This could be a valid response and happens in the real exam. Check your answer against the Study Text to make sure that this is correct before moving on to the next section of the notes.

Once you have completed the Key Fact Tests, move on to the Question Bank and then the Mock Exams.

Mock Exams

The Mock Exams are based on questions in the real exams. They are not exact reproductions of exam questions, but provide an accurate impression of the real thing. You should attempt the papers under exam conditions, so that you gain experience of selecting and sequencing your questions, and managing your time. Applying our marking scheme will help you get an idea of how you will fare in your exam. Rework them until you are achieving a mark of around 80% to ensure you are well above the exam pass mark of around 55%.

TAX TABLES

INCOME TAX RATES

2001/02		2000/01	
Rate %	Band £	Rate %	Band £
10	0 - 1,880	10	0 – 1,520
22	1,881 - 29,400	22	1,521 – 28,400
40	Over 29,400	40	Over 28,400

NATIONAL INSURANCE CONTRIBUTIONS
2001/02 rates

	Weekly	Monthly	Yearly
Class I (employee)			
Lower Earnings Limit (LEL)	£72.00	£312.00	£3,744.00
Upper Earnings Limit (UEL)	£575.00	£2,492.00	£29,900.00

Employees' contributions – Class 1

Total earnings £ per week	Contracted in rate	Contracted out rate
Below £87.00★	Nil	Nil
£87.01 - £575.00	10%	8.4%

Employers' contributions – Class 1

Total earning £ per week	Contracted-in rate	Contracted-out rate	
		Final salary	Money purchase
Below £87.00★	Nil	Nil	Nil
£87.01 - £575.00	11.9%	8.9%	11.3%
Excess over £575.00	11.9%	11.9%	11.9%

★ Earnings threshold below which no NICs payable. There is a zero band between the lower earnings limit (£72 pw) and the earnings threshold (£87 pw) to protect lower earners' rights to contributory state benefits such as basic state pension.

Class 1A (employer's contributions on most benefits)   11.9% on all relevant benefits

Class II (self-employed)   Flat rate per week £2.00 where earnings are over £3,955 pa

Class III (voluntary)   Flat rate per week £6.75

Class IV (self-employed)   7% on profits £4,535 - £29,900

INCOME TAX RELIEFS

		2001/02 £	2000/01 £
Personal allowance	- under 65	4,535	4,385
	- 65 – 74	5,990	5,790
	- 75 and over	6,260	6,050
Married couple's allowance	- 65 – 74 (see note 1)	5,365	5,185
	- 75 and over (see note 1)	5,435	5,255
	minimum for 65+	2,070	2,000
Age allowance income limit		17,600	17,000
Widow's bereavement allowance (see Note 2)		-	2,000
Blind person's allowance		1,450	1,400
Enterprise investment scheme relief limit (see Note 3)		150,000	150,000
Venture capital trust relief limit (see Note 3)		100,000	100,000
Children's tax credit allowance (see Note 4)		5,200	-

Notes

1   Either spouse must be born before 6 April 1935.

2   WBA only available for 2000/01 if husband dies in 1999/00; relief restricted to 10%. No relief for 2001/02.

3   EIS and VCT qualify for 20% relief.

4   Children's tax credit restricted to 10% relief. The allowance is reduced by £2 for every £3 of income taxed at the higher rate.

PERSONAL PENSION CONTRIBUTIONS (PPCs) and RETIREMENT ANNUITY PREMIUMS (RAPs)

	% of Net Relevant Earnings	
Age at beginning of tax year	**PPCs** %	**RAPs** %
35 or less	17.5	17.5
36 – 45	20	17.5
46 – 50	25	17.5
51 – 55	30	20
56 – 60	35	22.5
61 or more	40	27.5

Earning limit (PPCs only)		
	2001/02	£95,400
	2000/01	£91,800
	1999/00	£90,600
	1998/99	£87,600
	1997/98	£84,000
	1996/97	£82,200
	1995/96	£78,600
	1994/95	£76,800
	1993/94	£75,000

CAR AND FUEL BENEFITS

Company cars	35% of list price (max £80,000 including VAT).
2001/02	Reduce by ¼ for cars at least 4 years old at end of tax year

Car fuel scale		Up to 1400cc	1401-2000cc	Over 2000cc
2001/02 –	petrol	1,930	2,460	3,620
	diesel	2,460	2,460	3,620
2000/01 –	petrol	1,700	2,170	3,200
	diesel	2,170	2,170	3,200

Further information:

(a) **Car benefit** is reduced to 25% of list price where business miles are at least 2,500 p.a. and to 15% where business miles are at least 18,000 p.a.

(b) **In most cases, accessories** are included in the list price on which the benefit is calculated.

(c) **List price** is reduced by employee's capital contributions (maximum £5,000).

(d) **Car benefit** is reduced by the amount of employee's contributions towards running costs, but **fuel scale** benefit is reduced only if the employee makes good **all** the fuel used for private journeys.

FIXED PROFIT CAR SCHEME
(AUTHORISED MILEAGE RATES)

2001/02 rates	Up to 1,500cc	1501-2000cc	Over 2000cc
Up to 4,000 miles	40p	45p	63p
Over 4,000 miles	25p	25p	36p

Flat rate -	Up to 4,000 miles	40p
(all sizes)	Over 4,000 miles	22.5p

INHERITANCE TAX

Death rate	Lifetime rate	Chargeable 2001/02	Chargeable 2000/01
%	%	£'000	£'000
Nil	Nil	0 – 242	0 – 234
40	20	Over 242	Over 234

Reliefs

Annual exemption	£3,000	Marriage	- parent	£5,000
Small gifts	£250		- grandparent	£2,500
			- bride/groom	£2,500
			- other	£1,000

Reduced charge on gifts within 7 years of death

Years before death	0 - 3	3 - 4	4 - 5	5 - 6	6 – 7
% of death charge	100%	80%	60%	40%	20%

MAIN SOCIAL SECURITY BENEFITS

		From 9.4.01	From 10.4.00
		£	£
Child benefit	- first child	15.50	15.00
	- subsequent child	10.35	10.00
Incapacity benefit	- short term lower rate	52.60	50.90
	- short term higher rate	62.20	60.20
	- long term rate	69.75	67.50
Personal expenses allowance		16.05	15.45
Retirement provision	- single	72.50	67.50
	- married	115.90	107.90
Widowed parent's allowance		72.50	67.50
Bereavement payment (lump sum)		2,000.00	1,000.00

VALUE ADDED TAX

Standard Rate	17½%
Annual Registration Limit – from 1 April 2001	£54,000

CORPORATION TAX

Financial Year   **2000 to 31.3.01**
                            and 2001 to 31.3.02

Full rate	30%
Small companies rate	20%
Starting rate	10%
Profit limit for starting rate	£10,000
Effective marginal rate for starting rate	22.5%
Profit limit for starting rate	£50,000
Small companies limit	£300,000
Effective marginal rate for small companies	32.5%
Upper marginal limit	£1,500,000

BPP PUBLISHING

CAPITAL ALLOWANCES

	First year allowance	Writing down allowance pa
Plant and machinery	40% ★	25% (reducing balance)
Motor cars	-	25% (reducing balance) (max £3,000)
Industrial buildings	-	4% (straight line)
Agricultural buildings	-	4% (straight line)
Hotels	-	4% (straight line)
Enterprise Zones	100%	-
Scientific research	100%	-

★ For small and medium sized enterprises from 2 July 1998 (now permanent)

CAPITAL GAINS TAX

	2001/02	2000/01
Rate	Gains taxed at 10%, 20% or 40%, subject to level of income	Gains taxed at 10%, 20% or 40%, subject to level of income
Individuals-exemption	£7,500	£7,200
Trusts-exemption	£3,750	£3,600

TAPER RELIEF

(for disposals on or after 6 April 2000)

Gains on business assets		Gains on non-business assets ★	
Complete years after 5 April 98	% of gain chargeable	Complete years after 5 April 98	% of gain chargeable
0	100.0	0	100
1	87.5	1	100
2	75.0	2	100
3	50.0	3	95
4 or more	25.0	4	90
		5	85
		6	80
		7	75
		8	70
		9	65
		10 or more	60

★ Non-business assets held on 17 March 1998 given additional year of relief.

PHASING OUT RETIREMENT RELIEF

	100% relief on gains up to	**50% relief on gains between**
1999/2000	£200,000	£200,001 - £800,000
2000/2001	£150,000	£150,001 - £600,000
2001/2002	£100,000	£100,001 - £400,000
2002/2003	£50,000	£50,001 - £200,000

RETAIL PRICES INDEX

	Jan	Feb	Mar	Apr	May	Jun	Jul	Aug	Sep	Oct	Nov	Dec
1982			79.4	81.0	81.6	81.9	81.9	81.9	81.9	82.3	82.7	82.5
1983	82.6	83.0	83.1	84.3	84.6	84.8	85.3	85.7	86.1	86.4	86.7	86.9
1984	86.8	87.2	87.5	88.6	89.0	89.2	89.1	89.9	90.1	90.7	91.0	90.9
1985	91.2	91.9	92.8	94.8	95.2	95.4	95.2	95.5	95.4	95.6	95.9	96.0
1986	96.2	96.6	96.7	97.7	97.8	97.8	97.5	97.8	98.3	98.5	99.3	99.6
1987	100.0	100.4	100.6	101.8	101.9	101.9	101.8	102.1	102.4	102.9	103.4	103.3
1988	103.3	103.7	104.1	105.8	106.2	106.6	106.7	107.9	108.4	109.5	110.0	110.3
1989	110.0	111.8	112.3	114.3	115.0	115.4	115.5	115.8	116.6	117.5	118.5	118.8
1990	119.5	120.2	121.4	125.1	126.2	126.7	126.8	128.1	129.3	130.3	130.0	129.9
1991	130.2	130.9	131.4	133.1	133.5	134.1	133.8	134.1	134.6	135.1	135.6	135.7
1992	135.6	136.3	136.7	138.8	139.3	139.3	138.8	138.9	139.4	139.9	139.7	139.2
1993	137.9	138.8	139.3	140.6	141.0	141.0	140.7	141.3	141.9	141.8	141.6	141.9
1994	141.3	142.1	142.5	144.2	144.7	144.7	144.0	144.7	145.0	145.2	145.3	146.0
1995	146.0	146.9	147.5	149.0	149.6	149.8	149.1	149.9	150.6	149.8	149.8	150.7
1996	150.2	150.9	151.5	152.6	152.9	153.0	152.4	153.1	153.8	153.8	153.9	154.4
1997	154.4	155.0	155.4	156.3	156.9	157.5	157.5	158.5	159.3	159.5	159.6	160.0
1998	159.5	160.3	160.8	162.6	163.5	163.4	163.0	163.7	164.4	164.5	164.4	164.4
1999	163.4	163.7	164.1	165.2	165.6	165.6	165.1	165.5	166.2	166.5	166.7	167.3
2000	166.6	167.5	168.4	170.1	170.7	171.1	170.5	170.5	171.7	171.6	172.1	172.2
*2001	172.5	173.0	173.5	174.0	174.5	175.0	175.5	176.0	176.5	177.0	177.5	178.0
*2002	178.5	179.0	179.5	180.0	180.5	181.0	181.5	182.0	182.5	183.0	183.5	184.0

* Assumed.

Indexation relief was frozen at 5 April 1998 and replaced by taper relief for individuals and trustees.

BPP PUBLISHING

Key Facts
Questions

1   STATE PENSION SCHEME AND SERPS

1.1   What assumptions are made by the DSS in their forecast of an individual's SERPS benefits?

1.2   Which elements of the state pension can be topped up with Class 3 voluntary contributions and what are the main conditions that apply?

1.3   Explain the treatment of periods with no National Insurance Contributions, where the individual was not working, but looking after their children.

1.4   How can going to University affect an individual's entitlement to Basic State Pension?

1.5   Explain how a man's retirement after age 60, but before age 65 would affect his National Insurance Contributions record.

1.6   How will the State Retirement Age of Women be affected by the provisions of the Pensions Act 1995?

1.7   How can an individual get an accurate forecast of his/her State Retirement Benefits?

2   APPROVAL BY THE PENSIONS SCHEMES OFFICE AND TAX TREATMENT OF PENSIONS

2.1   List the beneficial tax features of an approved personal pension scheme.

2.2   In the context of UK based arrangements:

(i)   Describe the taxation implications for the employer, the employees and the assets of a contributory exempt approved occupational pension scheme.

(ii)   State the principal differences in tax treatment between an exempt approved occupational pension scheme and

(1)   An unfunded, unapproved scheme
(2)   A funded, unapproved scheme

2.3   What are the conditions for approval under Section 590?

3   PERSONAL PENSIONS AND RETIREMENT ANNUITY PLANS

3.1   At what rate does the earnings cap rise?

3.2   Outline the types of permitted investment for a Self Invested Personal Pension.

3.3   List the main features relating to the flexibility and level of pension income for personal pension fund withdrawals and personal pension phased retirement.

3.4   How many years is it possible to carry back a pension contribution?

3.5   Give six sources of earnings which are not relevant for the purposes either of Personal Pensions or of Retirement Annuity Plans (Section 226 policies).

3.6   What conditions must apply if an employer wishes to contribute to a Retirement Annuity Plan?

3.7   Give two sources of earnings which are 'Relevant' for a Retirement Annuity, but not for a Personal Pension.

4   OCCUPATIONAL SCHEMES

4.1   List the investments which require the SSAS administrators to notify the PSO within 90 days of them taking place.

4.2   What are the rules governing a company investing in its own shares via a SSAS?

4.3   List the rules relating to SSAS lending.

4.4   What are the rules relating to SSAS borrowing?

4.5   What are the main Inland Revenue conditions that apply for deferment of annuity purchase with a SSAS?

4.6   List the types of Schemes governed by Inland Revenue maximum benefit rules.

4.7   To whom must basic Occupational Pension scheme details be provided either automatically or on request under the Disclosure of Information Regulations 1986?

4.8   What restrictions are there on controlling directors joining or contributing to:

(a)   A Personal Pension Plan?
(b)   An Executive Pension Plan?

4.9   Explain *two* possible methods for funding a money purchase Occupational Scheme that provides benefits broadly similar to a final salary arrangement, but without the same level of guarantees.

5   DOCTORS AND DENTISTS

5.1   What are the retirement planning options open to a GP who is a member of the NHSPS and has no private practice earnings available?

5.2   What is the substance of Extra-statutory Concession A9?

6   ADDITIONAL CONTRIBUTIONS

6.1   What are the main considerations when advising a client whether to join the in-house AVC or to take out an FSAVC?

6.2   Under what circumstances can an AVC/FSAVC be used to increase an individual's tax free cash at retirement?

6.3   How many AVC and/or FSAVC arrangements is it possible to contribute to?

7   UNAPPROVED ARRANGEMENTS

7.1   Summarise the taxation of a FURBS.

7.2   How are Death-In-Service benefits taxed under a FURBS?

8   TRANSFERS

8.1   For which financial features might you need to make assumptions when advising of the value of two pensions options (eg to transfer or not to transfer)?

8.2   Why must these assumptions (in 8.1) be consider together rather than in isolation?

8.3   What financial assumptions are required by the PIA for use in a transfer value analysis?

8.4   Other than the produced critical yield, what factors should you consider when advising on the suitability of a transfer?

8.5   What effect would each of the following have on the critical yield of a transfer analysis?

     (a)   An increased Annuity Interest Rate

     (b)   An increased assumption for price inflation

8.6   What information could you obtain from a scheme booklet? When advising an individual, how reliable is the booklet he/she provides?

8.7   What are the main considerations when deciding whether to transfer a final salary transfer value into a personal pension plan?

8.8   Explain the normal conditions that must be fulfilled in order to allow an overseas pension to be transferred into a UK personal pension scheme or a UK occupational scheme.

BPP PUBLISHING

Key Facts
Answers

1   STATE PENSION SCHEME AND SERPS

1.1   *DWP assumptions*

The forecast of SERPS benefit is based on a projection of current earnings and status.

If earnings increase in the future, the benefit will be *higher* than forecast.

If earnings decrease in the future, the benefit will be *lower* than forecast.

If the individual contracts out, they will accrue no further SERPS entitlement and the benefits will be *lower* than forecast.

If the individual becomes self-employed, no further SERPS benefit will accrue and the benefits will be *lower* than forecast.

1.2   *Class 3*

Class 3 contributions can only be used to increase Basic State pension.

Voluntary contributions can only be used to make up any NIC deficit in the previous 6 years.

Voluntary contributions do not increase the pension above the maximum.

Contributions must be made before state retirement age.

1.3   They will receive the Home Responsibilities Protection (HRP) allowance.

This will improve their NIC record, which may improve their Basic State Pension.

HRP gives credit for years spent at home with dependant children (receiving child benefit).

1.4   Basic State pension is based on Class 1 and Class 2 NI contributions paid during an individual's working life.

This is defined as running from age 16 to the State retirement age.

To qualify for the full Basic State pension the individual must have NI credits for at least 90% of this time.

Many people go to university from age 18-21, removing 3 or more years from their NI contribution record. Any further losses would result in even greater reductions in their Basic State pension.

1.5   It would not!

The NI record for an individual will be automatically credited from the tax year in which they reach age 60 to the tax year before they reach 65.

If they do not earn sufficient to pay Class 1 or Class 2 NI, they will be credited as having paid them.

1.6   The provisions seek to equalise the pension benefits of men and women.

It affects women born after 5 April 1950.

Women born on or after 6 April 1955 will have a State retirement age of 65.

Women born between 6 April 1950 and 5 April 1955 will have a State retirement age that falls between age 60 and 65.

1.7   Complete form BR19.

Return the form to the DWP headquarters in Newcastle.

The DWP will send out a comprehensive statement that provides a breakdown of State pension entitlement, including current and future projections for Basic Pension, SERPS and Graduated Pension.

2   **APPROVAL BY THE IR SPSS* TAX TREATMENT OF PENSIONS**

* *Note*: Inland Revenue Savings, Pensions, Share Schemes has absorbed the former Pension Schemes Office (PSO).

2.1   *Taxation of Personal Pensions*

There is tax relief on member's contributions at highest marginal rate.

£3,600 gross may be paid without reference to earnings, and payments will be net of basic rate tax, even for non-earners.

Above £3,600 gross contributions, contributions are up to a percentage of net relevant earnings in any of the current or five preceding tax years. The year selected is the 'basis year' and the earnings cap for that year applies.

Unused tax relief from earlier years cannot be carried forward after 2000/01.

Contributions can be carried back to the previous year only and tax relief obtained against that year's pay. The election must be made by the time the contribution is made, and in any event by 31 January in the tax year.

No tax is paid by an employee on an employer's contributions (not treated as a benefit in kind).

Investments are free of tax on income and capital gains, but the tax credit on UK dividends cannot be reclaimed.

Lump sums paid on death are free of income tax.

Lump sums paid on death are free of inheritance tax if paid at the discretion of trustees.

Lump sums at retirement are tax free within limits.

2.2   (i)   *Taxation of Occupational Pension Schemes*

Employer

Contributions are deductible as a business expense.

Relief is immediate for regular contributions, but may have to be deferred for large special contributions.

Contributions do not attract any liability to pay NICs.

Any refund of surplus from the scheme is taxed at a free standing rate of 40% with no allowable off-sets.

Employee

Employer's contributions are not assessable to income tax as a benefit in kind on the employee.

Employees' regular and voluntary contributions are fully deductible for income tax purposes at the employee's highest marginal rate up to a maximum of 15% of taxable remuneration (limited by the Earnings Cap).

Employees' contributions do not escape NICs.

Pensions on retirement or death in service are taxed as earned income. No NICs are payable.

Cash at retirement is free of tax provided the amount is within approvable limits.

Cash on death in service or on death after retirement is not subject to inheritance tax or income tax provided it is payable at the trustees' discretion and the amounts are within approved limits.

Alternatively, they are payable to legal personal representatives and may attract inheritance tax.

No tax paid on the capital growth arising from the investment of employees' voluntary contributions.

For leavers with less than two years' service, personal contributions (with or without interest) may be refunded with a tax deduction of 20%.

Surplus voluntary contributions refunded to the member are subject to a penal tax.

All benefit payments are subject to limits specified by the Inland Revenue failure to observe these limits will result in loss of tax status for the scheme.

Assets

All capital gains and investment income are free of all taxes, although tax deducted on UK equity dividends is not reclaimable in addition to certain overseas withholding taxes.

If scheme surplus exceeds limits prescribed by the Inland Revenue and action is not taken to remove that surplus over a five-year period, the Inland Revenue can assess part of the investment earnings of the scheme to tax.

(ii)   *Taxation of Unfunded Unapproved Schemes*

Employer

Deductibility of tax is deferred until payment is made.

Employee

There are no limits on the benefit that can be paid.

All benefits, including death in service lump sums, are taxable as income at the time they are received.

Provided the scheme is sponsored by the employer and death in service cash is distributed at the trustees' discretion then lump sums on death are not assessable to inheritance tax.

Taxation of Funded Unapproved Schemes

Employer

If there is a funded unapproved group life scheme, there may be a chargeable gain on a second death claim.

Employer contributions are subject to NICs.

Employee

The employer's contributions are assessable to income tax as a benefit in kind on the member.

Benefits paid as a lump sum on retirement are free from income tax (without limit).

Death in service benefits (without limit) are not liable to inheritance tax subject to the proviso outlined in Part (ii)(a).

Personal contributions are not deductible for income tax purposes.

Assets

The assets are subject to tax on income and capital gains.

Tax on investment earnings is generally restricted to the basic rate of income tax.

11

2.3 Pension cannot start earlier than age 60 or later than age 75.

Maximum accrual rate is 1/60th for each year (maximum 40 years).

The only death benefits allowed are survivor pensions for death after retirement.

The maximum commutation of pension for tax free cash is at 3/80ths for each year of service (maximum of 40 years).

3   PERSONAL PENSIONS AND RETIREMENT ANNUITY PLANS

3.1 Increased in line with the Retail Prices Index
Rounded to the nearest £600
Increased each year through the Finance Act
This increase is not automatic

3.2 Stocks and shares
Futures and options
Depository interests
Unit trusts
OIEC shares
Insurance policies
Travel endowment policies
Deposits in any currency
Commercial property
Residential property linked to employment, such as a caretaker's flat
Ground rents

3.3 *Pension fund withdrawals*

If tax free cash is to be taken, it must be taken at outset. Once 'income' commences, no tax free cash can be taken.

The income taken can be varied within the Government Actuary Department (GAD) limits.

The GAD limits are linked to the single life annuity rates for the client's age, based on 15 year Gilt yields.

The minimum income is 35% of the GAD maximum.

These limits are reviewed every three years, at which time the income must be set within the revised limits. The fund can be used to purchase an annuity, via the open market option, at any time. An annuity must be purchased before the member reaches age 75.

Phased retirement

A client's fund is divided into a number of identical smaller policies that can be encashed as required – hence varying the income.

Annuities once purchased must be payable for life.

Any number of the smaller individual policies can remain invested until age 75 – by which time annuities must be purchased.

Income can be provided by the annuity or tax free cash or, most commonly, by a combination of the two.

Each time an annuity is purchased, a decision must be made as to the level of guarantee and/or spouse's pension. Once chosen for a particular number of the smaller policies being encashed, this cannot be altered.

3.4 One year, subject to election by the time the contribution is made and by 31 January at the latest.

3.5   Investment income

State benefits (excluding Enterprise Allowances)

Pension benefits in payment

Earnings from employment in respect of which the individual is a member of an occupational pension scheme that provides for retirement benefits.

Earnings from an investment company where the individual is a Controlling Director

Income benefits from personal PHI contracts

3.6   The employer cannot contribute directly to a Retirement Annuity.

The employer can increase the employee's salary.

This will allow the employee to make the contribution to the Retirement Annuity.

The increased salary will give rise to further employer NI contributions and possibly increased employee NI contributions.

3.7   Income from share option schemes.

The taxable element of golden handshakes, redundancy payments and approved ex-gratia payments.

4   OCCUPATIONAL SCHEMES

4.1   Making a loan to the employer or an associated company

Buying or selling land or property

Borrowing

Buying or selling the shares of an unlisted company

Buying or selling shares in the employer company or a company associated with the employer

Buying, selling or leasing other assets from or to the company or an associated company

4.2   The company cannot buy shares from a member or 'connected' person.

The maximum shareholding is limited to 30% in a private company.

The maximum portion of the fund that may be invested in this way is limited to 25% of the fund (excluding the fund derived from transfers) during the first two years of the SSAS, and 50% of the fund thereafter. Any loans from the SSAS to the employer are added in for this purpose.

4.3   Loans limited to 25% of the fund value in the first two years of the SSAS.

Loans limited to 50% of the fund value after two years of the SSAS.

Must exclude funds earmarked for providing benefits for a member who has retired for those who are drawing a pension from the fund.

Must exclude the fund derived from transfers made into the SSAS during the first two years of the SSAS.

The loan must be used for business purposes only eg purchase of plant, equipment, or of commercial property.

The term of the loan must be fixed.

The term must be appropriate for the purpose of the loan.

The Inland Revenue (IR) will normally have no objection to a loan being 'rolled over' but not normally more than twice.

The interest rate on the loan should be at a commercial rate (base +3%), unless it can be clearly demonstrated that the money would be available at a lower rate elsewhere.

4.4 45% of the market value of the fund.

Must exclude funds earmarked for providing benefits for a member who has retired and for those who are drawing a pension from the fund.

plus three times the employer's ordinary annual contributions

plus three times the member's annual contributions (excluding any voluntary contributions)

There must be a commercial reason for the borrowing.

The IR should be notified within 90 days, except where the loan is for less than six months or the amount borrowed is less than £50,000 or 10% of the current market value of the fund.

4.5 The members receive a pension income that is within 10% of that available if an annuity were to be purchased.

The annuity must be purchased by the 75th birthday.

The trustees and actuary must regularly review the annuity market.

If scheme assets are invested in property, there must be sufficient liquid assets for the annuity to be purchased within five years of the appropriate date (retirement age, or age 75 where drawdown is used).

The deferring member's fund cannot be used for loans to the employer or to purchase employer's shares, or be counted in the borrowing calculations.

4.6 Final Salary Schemes
COMPs
CIMPS
Executive Pensions
Small Self-Administered Schemes
AVCs

4.7 Members
Prospective Members
Spouses
Beneficiaries
Recognised independent Trade Unions

4.8 (a) Someone in an occupational pension scheme who is a controlling director or who has been a controlling director in any of the previous five tax years (disregarding years before 2000/01) may not contribute to a personal pension plan.

(b) Controlling directors of investment companies are not eligible for EPP membership.

They may not take out FSAVCs.

Their spouses may not be members of the EPP unless the Inland Revenue is satisfied that they are 'real' employees of the company.

4.9   The two methods are:

- Targeted money purchase
- Tiered contributions scheme

Targeted money purchase

These schemes aim to provide a pension calculated using a final salary formula, with benefits depending on the money purchase basis.

The pensions being offered are not guaranteed and will depend on the fund performance and annuity rates at retirement.

Regular reviews are carried out and contributions can be increased, although there is no obligation to do so.

Tiered contribution schemes

Contributions increase with age and/or service.

These schemes aim to offer higher contributions as the term to retirement gets shorter.

Benefits are not guaranteed but will depend upon fund performance and annuity rates at retirement.

5   DOCTORS AND DENTISTS

5.1   The options are:

- Invest in the NHS in-house AVC arrangement

- Purchase additional service through the 'added years' route

- Invest in a Free Standing Additional Voluntary Contribution plan

- Forego income tax relief on the NHSPS contributions and invest in a Personal Pension, while remaining a member of the NHS Scheme

5.2   It allows doctors and dentists who are taxed under Schedule D (self employed) to be members of the NHSPS and also to contribute to a Personal Pension.

6   ADDITIONAL CONTRIBUTIONS

6.1   Although this area tends to highlight client specific-issues, the following list would gain full marks.

If earning below £30,000 and not a controlling director, the client should consider contributing up to the limit of £3,600 pa gross in a stakeholder or other personal pension scheme, which will provide a 25% tax-free lump sum.

Is there an 'added years' option that would be beneficial if the client thinks their income is likely to rise well in excess of inflation?

Is the employer willing to match contributions to the in-house AVC?

Is the client a higher rate tax payer likely to benefit from the advantages of immediate relief under the in-house AVC?

The difference in charges between the AVC and FSAVC.

What are the investment fund options available through each arrangement?

Is the client likely to become a controlling director and be unable to continue the FSAVC?

When does the client wish to retire?

Is the issue of privacy important to the client?

Will the client be moving job again?

Does the in-house AVC arrangement offer additional benefits such as spouse's pension and/or escalation?

6.2 AVC arrangements entered into before 8 April 1987 can be used directly to increase tax free cash.

Schemes after this date may only provide retirement income benefits.

AVCs on an 'added years' basis will be increasing both pension and cash entitlement.

FSAVCs and AVCs linked to post-1989 membership may increase the tax free cash benefits by virtue of the formula 2.25 × initial pension that is used by the main scheme. The initial pension figure will *include* the FSAVC/AVC benefits.

6.3 Only one FSAVC per tax year.

As many AVCs as are available.

Contributions can be made to both an AVC and FSAVC at the same time as long as maximum contributions or benefits are not exceeded.

7   UNAPPROVED ARRANGEMENTS

7.1 The employer's contribution is treated as a benefit in kind. The return is made in the form of a P11D. It is collected via self assessment and a change to tax coding.

There is a NIC liability on the employer's FURBS contribution.

The funds are subject to tax on investment income and capital gains.

The benefits are free of income tax to the employee if they are paid as a lump sum.

Offshore FURBS build up funds free of tax, but the benefits are potentially taxable when paid to the employee (for funds started or varied after 30 November 1993).

7.2 The premium is taxable as a benefit in kind (as with other contributions).

The proceeds of individual policies are paid tax-free. The claim triggers a chargeable event, but as there is no surrender value prior to death there will not be a tax charge.

Where an unapproved Group Life scheme is used, there is an anomaly caused by the fact that it is not an exempt approved scheme. The chargeable event taxes the surrender value before death (usually nil) and the benefits are paid out, less premiums.

Where more than one death occurs, a tax charge may arise. This anomaly is easily avoided by using individual life policies rather than a group scheme.

8   TRANSFERS

8.1 Investment return
Salary growth
Price inflation
Level of discretionary pension increases
Annuity interest rates

8.2 Annuity interest rate

8.3 Salary growth (ie 1½% less than the annuity interest rate)
Price inflation (ie 3% less than the annuity interest rate)

8.4 Differences between pension increases allowed for in the transfer amount and those that may be paid in the future.

Differences in risk characteristics of the deferred pension and the various transfer destinations.

8.5 Higher AIR (in isolation) means lower critical yield.
Higher price inflation (in isolation) means higher critical yield.

8.6 (a) Name of scheme

Address of scheme administrator or other contact

Details of benefits provided in respect of current employer (eg death in service)

Details of benefits provided to early leavers (eg deferred pension)

Details of benefits provided on retirement (eg pension, lump sum)

Details of discretionary increases during last five years

Details of eligibility for membership and contributions payable

(a) Not too reliable

- Could be out of date
- Could be on special benefit terms

A benefit statement or other confirmation from the scheme administrator will usually be necessary.

8.7 Retirement flexibility

Charges under the personal pension scheme

The client's attitude to investment risk and the critical yield

The loss of final salary guarantees

Tax free cash entitlement

Death benefits

The range of investment funds available under the Personal Pension and their performance

Disability benefits

8.8 *Transfer to a personal pension scheme*

The client must be making contributions to the personal pension.

The client must have been employed abroad for at least two years.

PSO approval will be required in all cases.

Transfer to an occupational pension scheme

The client must be an active member of the scheme.

The client must have been employed abroad for at least two years.

Inland Revenue (SPSS) approval will be required.

Exam Question Bank

SECTION A

A1   Explain briefly the current and future rules applicable to those who choose to delay taking their State Pension Benefit beyond State Retirement Age.   **(7 marks)**

A2   Certain limitations apply with regard to self-investment where a company has established a small self-administered scheme (SSAS).

Identify those limitations where the company wishes to borrow back from the SSAS.

(7 marks)

A3   Tony Armstrong is a 40% taxpayer and is retiring at the age of 60. He has been advised by his pension advisers that his Free-Standing AVC is 'over-funded' to the tune of £12,000.

Explain and calculate the tax charge applicable to the over-funded amount.   **(7 marks)**

A4   Identify the main differences between Retirement Annuity Plans and Personal Pension Plans.   **(8 marks)**

A5   Detail the tax concessions applicable to contributions to a Personal Pension plan. **(6 marks)**

A6   Compare Individual Savings Accounts and Personal Pension Plans in the event of death before benefits are taken.   **(7 marks)**

A7   List the main features of the Civil Service Pension Scheme in relation to:

(a)   Contributions   **(2 marks)**
(b)   Benefits at retirement   **(4 marks)**
(c)   Benefits on Death In Service   **(2 marks)**

A8   Why should an individual wish to take their full entitlement to tax free cash from their pension and use this to buy a purchased life annuity rather than take the whole fund in the form of pension? (You should assume that this individual will pay tax at the basic rate after retirement.)   **(5 marks)**

A9   A 65 year old man is about to retire when he comes to see you for some advice on how to take his pension in retirement. He currently has a Retirement Annuity Fund of £100,000 which would provide a pension of £7,000 and a tax free sum. His objective is to get the maximum tax free cash on retirement. He could use the Open Market Option via a Personal Pension Plan. Bearing in mind the clients objective, what would be your recommendation and why?   **(5 marks)**

A10   Brian has been drawing a pension under the fund withdrawal scheme. However he dies aged 69. Outline the options his 65 year-old widow will have under the Income Withdrawal rules.

(5 marks)

A11   Assuming a FURBS has been established following Inland Revenue recommendations, describe the tax treatment of the FURBS. (You should ignore National Insurance Contributions in your answer.)   **(5 marks)**

A12   Stephen has worked for a private bank for the last four years and is a member of a non-contributory final salary scheme. During his service he has contributed to an FSAVC. What are his options with the FSAVC fund given the fact that he is due to leave his employer in the near future?   **(5 marks)**

A13 Explain the rules applicable to the timing of taking benefits from a personal pension scheme where there are no protected rights benefits. **(5 marks)**

A14 Identify the main changes that apply to contracting-out using contracted-out money purchases (COMPs) as a consequence of the Pensions Act 1995. **(5 marks)**

A15 Martin is a member of a Small Self Administered Scheme and is about to retire. He has been advised that he does not have to purchase his pension immediately. Explain to him how he may take an income from the fund, and whether there are any limitations on how long he can do this. (You should assume that the Scheme operates the pre-June 1999 drawdown arrangements.) **(5 marks)**

A16 If the member of an occupational scheme is not a Controlling Director or a high earner, there are two definitions of final pay that the scheme may utilise. Outline each of them. **(5 marks)**

A17 The Minimum Funding requirement was introduced in the Pension Act 1995 to ensure that defined benefit schemes have sufficient assets to meet their liabilities at all times should the fund be wound up. What are the requirements of the Act with regard to this provision? **(5 marks)**

A18 Charles and Dora are to be divorced. Charles has been investing in a Personal Pension since July 1988 and has built up a substantial fund. He would like to know if this fund will be taken into account in the divorce settlement and if so what are the options. Advise Charles appropriately. **(5 marks)**

A19 Pink Computing is a small firm which had established a SSAS a year ago. At outset there was a contribution into the scheme of £60,000 by the employing company and recently a further £70,000. There have been no member contributions to the scheme.

Elliott, a director of the company transferred his personal pension fund of £100,000 into the scheme. The fund is currently valued at £250,000.

Calculate, showing all workings, the amount that the scheme would be allowed to borrow in order to purchase a commercial property under Inland Revenue rules. **(5 marks)**

A20 Compare SIPPs and SSASs in relation to property purchase. You should consider the following.

(a) Borrowing from a lender so that there are sufficient funds to purchase the property
(4 marks)

(b) How property with a residential element would be treated in each type of scheme
(4 marks)

(c) How joint ownership of the property would be treated in each type of scheme
(2 marks)

A21 For an employee who is a member of a UK occupational pension scheme but currently working abroad, what are the circumstances under which IR SPSS (formerly the PSO) will allow that employee to continue to accrue benefits in that scheme? **(5 marks)**

A22 Sam is a nurse at Holby General Hospital and has come to you for advice on his pension benefits. He is a member of the National Health Service Superannuation Scheme. He joined the scheme in 1995 when he was 25 and he will retire at age 60. His current salary is £21,000.
£22000

(a)   Estimate what benefits Sam will receive on retirement assuming that his salary remains at the current level.   **(2 marks)**

(b)   State the lump sum that would be payable were Sam to die before retirement.   **(1 mark)**

A23   It is currently October 2001 and Aisha Mottram is aged 38. She is single but has a financially dependent daughter. She has been looking after her daughter at home and in full time education for a number of years. Last year she found employment as a research chemist for a drug company. Her earnings for the 2000/2001 tax year were £25,000 and in 2001/2002 she will earn £31,000. There is no occupational pension scheme or other beneficial arrangement offered by her employer. She has no previous pension arrangements.

Sandy has read an article in a Sunday newspaper about the high cost of pension provision. In order to build a fund as quickly as possible, she would like to make the maximum single contribution for the current tax year. She also read that she has the option to take out life cover under the pension and receive tax relief. She would like to take as much life cover as possible. (Her daughter will be the beneficiary in the event of her death.)

(a)   State how the maximum amount of life cover will be determined for Sandy.
                                                                    (1 mark)

(b)   Calculate, showing all workings, the maximum contribution that Sandy can pay into her pension in the current tax year. (You should assume that she is to take the maximum amount of life cover available.)   **(6 marks)**

A24   Stephen works as a trainer. There are no pension arrangements made for employees by his employer. Stephen has taken out a personal pension and has decided that he will contract out of SERPS via an Appropriate Personal Pension. To do so he completed form APP1 in December 2001.

(a)   State the date or dates from which the election to contract out could be effective.
                                                                    (2 marks)

(b)   Under what circumstances would the DSS cease to pay rebates of National Insurance Contributions into Stephen's pension during his working life?   **(5 marks)**

A25   Brian is an employee of a bank earning £65,000 pa and is a member of the bank's money purchase occupational pension scheme, to which he contributes 6% of his salary. He has been advised that he could boost his pension provision by sacrificing £11,000 of salary in return for a higher contribution to the pension scheme from his employer.

Explain to Brian reasons why sacrificing £11,000 of his salary could enable him to enhance his pension.   **(4 marks)**

A26   The Department for Work and Pensions (formerly the DSS) require an individual to pay National Insurance Contributions for about 90% of their working life in order to qualify for a full basic state pension. Apart from paying National Insurance Contributions, how might an individual maintain a sufficient National Insurance record so that they may benefit from a full basic state pension in retirement?   **(4 marks)**

A27   State and explain in general terms the effect that a fall in gilt yields would have on a critical yield obtained from a transfer value analysis.   **(5 marks)**

A28   Sally Gunner is a 28 year old athlete. She has earnings of £150,000 for the 2001/2002 tax year. She has just started a personal pension plan.

(a) What is the maximum contribution that she could make in the current tax year? You should ignore carry back.   **(3 marks)**

(b) Sally wants to know what is the earliest age she can take benefits from her pension plan. Advise her.   **(1 mark)**

(c) What is the maximum age to which she could defer taking her benefits?   **(1 mark)**

A29 In respect of personal pensions fund withdrawal, explain the following.

(a) The factors that influence the level of income taken from the non-protected rights fund.   **(3 marks)**

(b) Peter has a fund value of £250,000 remaining after deduction of the tax-free cash entitlement. He has been given a Government Actuary's Department factor of £85. Calculate the maximum and minimum income withdrawal that Peter will be allowed to take?   **(2 marks)**

(c) State how often the income withdrawal figure must be reviewed for an individual who has one of these plans.   **(1 mark)**

A30 Below is a list of birth dates for women. You should state for each whether they will receive their state pension at age 60, 65 or at an age in between.

(a) 5 March 1953   **(1 mark)**
(b) 7 January 1958   **(1 mark)**
(c) 19 October 1949   **(1 mark)**
(d) 25 March 1955   **(1 mark)**

A31 Where a contracted-out personal pension fund has received a transfer value from an Occupational Pension Scheme, state the effect that this will have on how the fund is paid out on death before retirement:

(a) Where there is a surviving spouse at the date of death   **(3 marks)**
(b) Where there is no surviving spouse at the date of death   **(2 marks)**

A32 For each of the following, explain how an employer's contribution would receive tax relief.

(a) A contribution to a personal pension plan   **(4 marks)**
(b) A Section 226 (Retirement Annuity Contract)   **(3 marks)**

A33 Jane earns £80,000 per annum. She has overfunded her FSAVC Scheme. The surplus has been calculated as £7,000. Calculate the following, showing your workings in full.

(a) The refund that would be paid by the FSAVC scheme   **(2 marks)**
(b) The total amount of tax that she will have to pay on the surplus?   **(4 marks)**

A34 List the methods that could be used to preserve the accrued benefits for the members of a contracted-out final salary scheme, where the scheme is to be wound up?   **(4 marks)**

A35 A client of yours is changing employment. He has come to you for pensions advice. He says that his new employer belongs to the same 'Transfer Club' as his existing employer.

(a) Explain to your client what is meant by the term 'Transfer Club'.   **(2 marks)**
(b) Why might your client want to take advantage of this facility?   **(3 marks)**

SECTION B

B1   Appleton Limited was formed by Graham Appleton, aged 50, in 1980 and his annual salary is £45,000. Graham's brother Robert is aged 47 and has a salary of £40,000. Robert joined the company in 1985, and Graham and Robert are controlling directors. John James, aged 35, joined the company in 1991 as Sales Manager and his salary is £30,000. Appleton Limited has been a profitable enterprise in recent years and substantial cash reserves are currently held on deposit.

The company does not have any existing Occupational Pension Scheme. Graham has, over the years, paid single premiums to a personal pension plan, which now has a fund value of £130,000, and there is no penalty in the event of a transfer value being taken.

Robert has a regular premium personal pension plan with a current fund value of £45,000 and a transfer value of £27,000.

John was a member of his former employer's contracted-out final salary pension scheme and has retained benefits in the scheme. John has recently received a transfer value quotation of £42,700 of which £13,400 represents GMP liability. Unused personal pension relief arising from his Appleton Limited earnings amount to £18,000.

Appleton Limited have been investigating the purchase of office premises and have been looking at an out-of-town development where they could purchase suitable accommodation for £195,000. They have asked you to advise them on a tax-efficient method of acquiring the property through pension arrangements.

(a)   Identify the options open to the company in respect of the property purchase.

(10 marks)

(b)   Explain the considerations which would determine how much money could be made available for the purchase by an approved pension scheme.   **(12 marks)**

(c)   Compare the rules and commercial considerations applicable to commercial and residential property purchase in respect of a SSAS and a SIPP.   **(27 marks)**

(d)   Detail the maximum funding rules as they apply to a SSAS.   **(26 marks)**

(Total 75 marks)

B2   Kevin would like advice regarding his pension arrangements. He is 46 at the beginning of October 2001. He has a wife, Sally, and two children, both under 10. He is considering retirement at age 55.

Kevin works for a publishing company on a salary of £45,000 per annum. He has worked for the company for two years and joined the Final Salary Company Pension scheme on joining the company.

The current scheme is set up as follows.

Accrual rate	1/60th
Normal Retirement Age	65
Pensionable salary	£45,000
Date of joining	1 December 1999

Kevin has worked for two other employers during his working life and has retained benefits with both.

First employer

Joined company	1 October 1981
Joined scheme	1 October 1984
Left employer	30 September 1990
Final pensionable salary	£20,000 pa
GMP accrued at leaving age	£1,950 pa
Accrual rate	1/60
Normal retirement age	65
GMP revaluation method	Fixed rate
Revaluation on the excess over the GMP is the statutory minimum basis	
Transfer value	£30,000

Second employer

Joined company and scheme	1 October 1990
Left company	30 September 1999
Final pensionable salary	£39,000
Golden handshake	£20,000
Average annual bonus	£10,000
Average benefits in kind	£2,500
Accrual rate	1/60
Normal retirement age	65
Contracted-in	
Fully indexed pension in payment and in deferment	
Transfer value	£60,000

(a) With reference to Kevin's retained benefits, answer the following questions.

    (i) Showing your workings, calculate the deferred pension that Kevin was entitled to at the date of leaving each scheme. **(2 marks)**

    (ii) With reference to the first employer's scheme, explain how to calculate the revalued pension at age 65. You should write about each of the stages in the calculation but you are not expected to do any calculations. **(10 marks)**

    (iii) State how the revalued pension would be calculated for Kevin's second employer's scheme. **(2 marks)**

(b) If Kevin wishes to consider transferring his retained benefits to his new employer's scheme:

    (i) State three benefit options the new employer's scheme may offer in return for the transfer value **(3 marks)**

    (ii) Outline two advantages and disadvantages of each of the options mentioned above

        (12 marks)

(c) Showing all workings, state the Inland Revenue maximum benefits for pension and tax-free cash. **(18 marks)**

(d) In each of the following scenarios, calculate the death benefits payable to Kevin's widow if he were to die soon after transferring.

    (i) Transfer takes place from the first employer's scheme to a Section 32 buy out bond.

        (4 marks)

(ii)   Transfer takes place from the first employer's scheme to a Personal Pension.

(5 marks)

(iii)   Transfer takes place from the second employer's scheme to a Section 32 buy-out bond.

(3 marks)

(iv)   Transfer takes place from second employer's scheme to a Personal Pension Plan.

(3 marks)

(e) As Kevin's adviser, explain the factors you would take into account in deciding between transferring to a Section 32 plan or a Personal Pension Plan.   **(13 marks)**

(Total 75 marks)

B3   Harry Fenner left First Millennium Packaging Ltd in December 2001. Harry, aged 48, had been a director of the company until March 1998, but a period of poor health forced him to take a less stressful role. At the same time, Harry sold his 30% shareholding in the business to the other directors.

Although Harry found his new role satisfactory, he felt fit and ready to take on new challenges. Harry joined a start-up firm of financial advisers which intends to focus on the internet as its main channel of distribution. Harry would ideally like to retire and take his pension benefits at age 60.

Harry was a member of First Millennium Packaging's contracted out and 60ths-based Final Salary scheme. The scheme's normal retirement age is 65. Harry had been in the scheme since January 1981 up to March 1998. Harry's final pensionable pay on leaving service was £110,000 pa.

(a) (i)   Calculate Harry's deferred pension at the date of leaving.   **(3 marks)**

(ii)   Describe how, and over what period the various elements of Harry's deferred pension will revalue between the date of leaving and normal retirement age. Calculations are not required.   **(12 marks)**

(b) Describe briefly the steps taken by the scheme actuary in calculating the transfer value stating the assumptions that are necessary for this purpose.   **(11 marks)**

(c) If Harry decided to transfer the value of his benefits in the First Millennium Packaging Ltd scheme to a personal pension scheme, explain the basis of and any restrictions applicable to the maximum tax free cash when benefits are taken. Calculations are not required.   **(13 marks)**

(d) If Harry were to transfer the value of his benefits in the First Millennium Packaging Ltd scheme to a personal pension, describe the nature of any other restrictions that may apply, stating why these restrictions are applicable.   **(19 marks)**

(e) If Harry were to transfer the value of his benefits in the First Millennium Packaging Ltd scheme to a Section 32 plan, describe the nature of any restrictions that may apply stating why these restrictions are applicable.   **(17 marks)**

(Total 75 marks)

B4   Cramer and Ermintrude Ltd operate a chain of retail shops selling high class cosmetic and other beauty products. The company has over 400 employees, many of who are part timers.

The company has operated a contracted out defined contribution occupational scheme since 1991. Membership of this scheme is restricted to head office staff, who in the main comprise the 30 strong management team.

For their remaining staff, Cramer and Ermintrude offer a group personal pension scheme where the company is willing to match member contributions subject to a maximum of 5% of basic pay.

(a) State the effects that the Pensions Act 1995 has had on:

    (i) The Cramer and Ermintrude Ltd contracted-out defined contribution occupational scheme **(17 marks)**

    (ii) The Cramer and Ermintrude Ltd group personal pension scheme **(4 marks)**

(b) If the company were to operate a defined benefit scheme for the entire workforce, what benefit conditions would need to be satisfied if the scheme were to contract out? **(12 marks)**

(c) John Cramer wishes to know more about his possible State Pension benefits at age 65.

    (i) Describe the conditions necessary for John to qualify for the full Basic State Pension. **(4 marks)**

    (ii) Explain how John might obtain a State Pension forecast and summarise the information shown in such a forecast. **(5 marks)**

(d) After taking advice Cramer and Ermintrude Ltd decide to discontinue the Defined Contribution Occupational Scheme and to adopt a strategy consistent with the approach used in the existing Group Personal Pension scheme for the workforce as a whole.

    (i) Describe the implications for the existing Defined Contribution Occupational Scheme members so far as future contracting out is concerned. **(6 marks)**

    (ii) What options will the existing Defined Contribution Occupational Scheme members have with regard to their benefits secured to date? **(6 marks)**

    (iii) In implementing the decided strategy what options are open to Cramer and Ermintrude Ltd with regard to ongoing benefit provision for the ex-Defined Contribution Occupational Scheme members. **(6 marks)**

(e) Harriet is a member of the Cramer and Ermintrude Ltd Group Personal Pension Scheme. Explain the options open to Harriet with regard to her benefits if she leaves service. **(9 marks)**

(f) List the circumstances in which Cramer and Ermintrude Ltd may wish to establish a FURBS for one or more its employees. **(6 marks)**

(Total 75 marks)

B5 You have been appointed as pensions adviser to Boyle and Bubble Ltd. The company has over 1,200 employees situated at various locations around the UK. The company already operates a Contracted-In Money Purchase Scheme where the company pay 3% of basic pay and requires a like contribution from the members. Employees are eligible to join the scheme after they have been employed for two years. The scheme is insured but only offers a with-profits fund. The performance track record of the provider is consistently below the average of with-profit providers generally.

Only 130 of the employees are in the money purchase scheme with the balance of the employees having decided not to join it, in many cases because they already have a personal pension plan of their own. Others are unattracted to the scheme because it is not well regarded by those in it and it is said that 'bad news spreads'.

The Managing Director of Boyle and Bubble Ltd asks you about the Government's reforms proposed to state pension provision and the introduction of stakeholder pensions. He wants to consider the impact of the Government's proposals on the company and its employees, whether or not they are in the existing scheme.

(a) Describe briefly the current structure of pension provision in the UK and the choices applicable to employees of Boyle and Bubble Ltd. **(25 marks)**

(b) Explain the effects of the Government's proposals for pensions reform on State pension provision and in particular how the proposals compare with the current provisions.

(22 marks)

(c) How is the introduction of stakeholder pensions likely to affect Boyle and Bubble Ltd and their employees, whether or not they are members of the existing pension scheme?

(28 marks)

(Total 75 marks)

SECTION C

C1   Geoff Keiller, now aged 41, accepted voluntary redundancy terms from his previous employer in December 1995, when his salary was £54,000 pa, and then set up in business in his specialist field of leak detection for the water industry.

Geoff's previous employer operated a contracted-in final salary pension scheme, giving a pension of $1/45^{th}$ of final pay for each complete year of membership with a 50% spouse's pension payable following death after retirement. The scheme anniversary is 1 March and has a normal retirement age of 60. The employer introduced the full requirements of limited price indexation on benefits accrued after 1 March 1992 in order to reduce scheme surplus.

Geoff joined service in November 1980, joining the pension scheme on the first scheme anniversary after a two year waiting period.

Geoff has received the offer to take a transfer value of £104,700 into either a Personal Pension or a Section 32 Buyout Plan. A transfer analysis has revealed that a critical yield of 7.8% is required to match the benefits from the occupational scheme.

Geoff's new business has grow dramatically as 2001 has progressed, following the action of the Water companies to detect and repair as many leaks as is feasible. Indeed, Geoff anticipates that his net relevant earnings for the 2001/2002 tax year will be as much as £120,000, whereas over the previous tax year he only had net relevant earnings of £24,000.

Geoff is keen to maximise his pension provision and intends to sell the business and retire when he is 50.

(a)   Calculate and explain Geoff's deferred pension benefits age 60 from the scheme of his previous employer.   **(12 marks)**

(b)   Explain and comment on the quoted critical yield.   **(5 marks)**

(c)   Geoff wants to retire at the age of 50. Explain how this might impact on any decision to take a transfer value into either a personal pension or a Section 32 plan.   **(10 marks)**

(d)   Assuming that a transfer is taken into a personal pension and that Geoff funds to the maximum possible over the period to age 50, explain how he can ensure that his benefits are taken so as to match his overall income requirements.   **(13 marks)**

(Total: 40 marks)

C2   Telephone Support Supplies Ltd wish to consider the option open to them in the provision of pensions for their senior executives. The company is concerned that it should properly consider all of the appropriate options as they have the overall objective of maximising benefits for this key group of senior executives.

As a consequence, the company wish to make sure that by a combination of arrangements, they are able to provide for equal benefits at a proposed retirement age of 60 for all of the individuals concerned in relation to their final earnings and irrespective of their years of service. All of the employees in this group will have at least five years service completed by the age of 60 and all have earnings in excess of £100,000 pa.

The individuals come from a variety of backgrounds and have past pension arrangements that vary in nature and extent dramatically, hence the employer's concern to ensure that an individual approach is adopted in order to meet the benefit objectives.

(a)   Identify the options open to the employer in making pension provision for this group, which may be used either separately or in combination.   **(4 marks)**

(b) Summarise the taxation considerations in respect of employee and employer contributions relevant to each of the identified options. **(12 marks)**

(c) Summarise the benefit constraints applicable to each of the options identified.

(11 marks)

(d) Summarise the tax treatment of the investments held within each of the options identified. **(6 marks)**

(e) Indicate how investments are held to ensure the security of benefits for the scheme members. **(7 marks)**

(Total: 40 marks)

C3   KNPS Training is a small training company. Its four founders, who are all directors, set it up as a limited company five years ago.

Four years ago, KNPS established a Small Self Administered Scheme (SSAS) for the benefit of the four directors.

The details of this scheme are as follows.

- The scheme started exactly four years ago.

- Fund value is £330,000 (including £80,000 of transfers-in received 3 years ago).

- Contributions to date are as follows.

Year	Employer	Employee
1	£43,000	£0
2	£57,000	£0
3	£65,000	£0

- The company wishes to buy its training premises using the SSAS to fund the purchase. The SSAS will then lease the property back to the company.

(a) What is the maximum amount that the Inland Revenue will allow the scheme to borrow?

Show how you arrive at this figure. **(17 marks)**

(b) What are the advantages for the scheme and the training company of the scheme purchasing the premises and then leasing it back to the company? **(10 marks)**

(c) State how the retirement pension may be provided from a SSAS. **(6 marks)**

(d) List and outline the conditions imposed by the Inland Revenue on loans from a SSAS to the sponsoring employer. **(7 marks)**

(Total: 40 marks)

C4   Penny Walker is aged 30 and married. She does not have any children at present but intends to start a family in the near future. She intends to continue working after having children.

Penny is a lawyer with a basic salary of £30,000. In addition, she benefits from a guaranteed bonus of 7% of her basic salary. The bonus is paid annually. Penny has other taxable benefits in kind of £1,500.

Penny joined her firm's contracted out final salary scheme when she started with them after qualifying as a lawyer. She joined on her 25th birthday.

The scheme details are as follows.

- Accrual rate is 1/60th.

- Penny contributes 6% of her basic salary.

- Pensionable pay is basic salary.

- Death in Service lump sum is three times pensionable pay plus a refund of member contributions.

- Death in Service spouse's pension is 50% of Penny's pensionable in service pension had she retired at NRD. In addition, a further 20% will be paid for children still in full-time education.

- Normal Retirement Date is age 60.

- Death After Retirement Pension for spouse is 50% of actual pension paid to Penny.

(a) Using Penny's current salary details, calculate, showing all your workings, what pension she would be entitled to if she remains with her current employers to age 60.

(2 marks)

(b) If Penny used an FSAVC to provide additional benefits on retirement or death, show in today's terms, what additional benefits she could provide. Show your workings in full.   **(29 marks)**

(c) The scheme that Penny belongs to is contracted-out. Explain how GMP accrual changed with effect from April 1997 and state the benefit basis that the scheme must now satisfy as a minimum.   **(9 marks)**

(Total: 40 marks)

C5   Chris is approaching his 53rd birthday and, due to the stresses and strains of his job, as a School Inspector of Languages, he would like to retire early. He believes that he will be able to work part-time on a consultancy basis with several schools because during his working life he has made a number of contacts which he can now call upon. Chris is not in an Occupational Pension scheme.

Chris has a personal pension fund of £568,000, which is currently invested in equity based funds. Chris is not contracted out of SERPS.

Chris expects to work part-time for the next five years. He will be looking to take the maximum tax-free cash from his fund to buy a retirement home in France and pay off his outstanding debts (a small mortgage of £15,000 on his home and £10,000 in unpaid credit cards). Chris comes to you for advice on how he can release enough cash to meet his needs and also provide additional income to top up his consultancy earnings should this be required.

(a) Suggest to Chris an arrangement which will meet his requirements and explain why you believe your suggestion is appropriate.   **(9 marks)**

(b) Calculate the maximum amount of cash that Chris can take from his personal pension fund.

State in general terms how this would differ if the pension plan were a retirement annuity and not a Personal Pension Plan. You should mention in your answer which plan could offer higher potential tax-free cash and why.   **(10 marks)**

(c) Consider the following extract from the Government Actuary's Department tables.

Age	5.0%	5.25%	5.50%	5.75%	6.0%
50	60	62	64	66	68
51	61	63	65	67	69
52	62	64	66	68	70
53	63	65	67	69	71
54	64	66	68	70	72
55	65	67	69	71	73

Given that the gilt yield is currently 5.6%, calculate the maximum *and* minimum income that Chris may draw if he uses this method. You should show all the steps in your calculation. **(8 marks)**

(d) Explain to Chris the *risks* associated with income drawdown as compared to purchasing an immediate annuity. **(9 marks)**

(e) Chris wants to know how his wife will be provided for should he die whilst drawing from the plan you have suggested. What would be the options for the surviving spouse on Chris's death before age 75? **(4 marks)**

(Total: 40 marks)

C6 Nigel has worked for Couch and Co Private Bank, the private banking arm of North West Bank Plc for the last three years. He is an executive with the bank, earning £85,000. He has joined the Couch and Co Staff Pension Scheme and they have also set up an Executive Pension Plan for him to provide additional benefits up to the Inland Revenue maximum.

Nigel joined Couch and Co from the Royal Bank of Caledonia. Details of his deferred pension benefits are shown below.

Name	Nigel Parker
Date of birth	1 April 1950
Date joining	1 June 1990
Date of leaving service	31 May 1997
Normal retirement age	65
Final pensionable pay on leaving	£60,000
Controlling Director?	No
Scheme basis	1/60th
Transfer value	£75,200
Including protected rights of	£6,655
GMP at date of leaving	£750
Revaluation method for GMP	Fixed
Excess of GMP revaluation basis	Statutory revaluation
Post-retirement pension increases	Limited Price Indexation

The critical yield has been calculated as 8.9% to normal retirement date on a transfer to a personal pension plan or section 32 buy-out bond.

(a) Showing your workings, calculate Nigel's deferred pension when he left the Royal Bank of Caledonia. **(4 marks)**

(b) Calculate the revalued pension to retirement date at age 65. You should assume that the RPI average increase is 5% per annum. **(9 marks)**

(c) Explain how the transfer value is calculated. Explain each stage in the process, including the considerations of the scheme actuary when determining the transfer value. **(15 marks)**

BPP PUBLISHING

(d)   Tabulate for both a personal pension plan and Section 32 buy-out bond the benefits that could be provided on Nigel's death before retirement. **(12 marks)**

(Total: 40 marks)

C7   Unapproved arrangements have become more popular since the Finance Act 1989 made it possible for someone to be a member of an Unapproved Arrangement and still enjoy the tax relief associated with an exempt approved arrangement.

(a)   Outline the reasons why an employer may wish to establish a FURBS, and state what benefits such an arrangement will have for the employees. **(16 marks)**

(b)   Explain the following.

    (i)   What is a FURBS? **(10 marks)**

    (ii)   What is an UURBS? **(8 marks)**

(c)   If an employee leaves the firm after three years service and has unapproved arrangements (UURBS and FURBS) what options are open to him? **(6 marks)**

(Total: 40 marks)

C8   John Hart aged 52 retired from HM Customs and Excise as a VAT Inspector, two years ago. He receives a pension of £25,000 per annum.

John decided to set up a VAT consultancy for small firms with his friend and colleague Ken MacDonald. The consultancy has done extremely well and both Ken and John now draw salaries of £70,000. They have recently incorporated their firm.

John has come to see you for professional retirement planning advice as he would like to retire in ten years time and he would like to know what are the best options available to him.

Ken and John have decided to buy the company premises from the landlord at what they believe is a reasonable price. They both think that property is a safe investment and a relatively good hedge against inflation. John wants to know if he could use his pension fund to help with the purchase cost.

(a)   How much could John currently contribute to a personal pension plan? **(2 marks)**

(b)   Excluding unapproved arrangements, outline to John the *two* main options open to company directors such as himself in terms of pension provision. **(17 marks)**

(c)   Bearing in mind that John wants to use his pension fund to purchase his business premises, which of the two alternatives would you recommend to John? **(8 marks)**

(d)   For each of the alternatives mentioned, state the rules relating to purchasing commercial property. **(13 marks)**

(Total: 40 marks)

Exam Answer Bank

SECTION A ANSWERS

A1   Both basic State Pension and SERPS may be deferred by a maximum of up to five years.

     2 marks

State Pension benefits increased during the period of deferment at the rate of 1/7th per cent in respect of each week of deferment.

     1 mark

This equals a 7.5% per annum rate of increase.

     1 mark

From 6 April 2010 the rate of increase of benefits into deferment changes to 10.4% per annum (1/5th percent per week).

     1 mark

With effect from 6 April 2010 the maximum deferment period of five years is abolished.

     1 mark

During deferment the only liability for further National Insurance Contributions is on the part of the employer.

     1 mark

     Total 7 marks

A2   Any loan from the SSAS to the principal employer must be for strictly commercial purposes.

     1 mark

Interest must be paid on the loan at a rate of 3% above base rate unless it can be shown that the company could borrow more cheaply from elsewhere.

     2 marks

The maximum loan is limited to 25% of fund excluding that relating to incoming transfer values in the first two years.

     2 marks

After the first two years, the maximum loan is restricted to 50% of fund value including that relating to incoming transfer values.

     2 marks

     Total 7 marks

A3   The over-funded amount will be refunded after the deduction of basic rate tax and a further 10% to take account of the tax-free fund growth enjoyed.

     2 marks

£12,000 × 32% = £3,840
£12,000 – £3,840 = £8,160

So the refund paid to Tony will be £8,160.

     1 mark

£8,160 × $^{100}/_{78}$ = £10,461.54

This is grossed up by basic rate tax to give £10,461.

     2 marks

The higher rate tax charge is 18% of £10,461.5$\cancel{6}$ = £1,883.08.

     1 mark

Therefore the net refund after all tax will be £6,276.92.

     1 mark

(*Note.* The easy way to check your answer is to apply 47.69% to the gross surplus. This gives the total tax charge where basic rate is 22% and higher rate is 40%.)

     Total 7 marks

A4   The permitted range of retirement ages with personal pension schemes is 50 - 75.

     1 mark

The permissible range of retirement ages with retirement annuities is age 60 - 75.

     1 mark

Contributions into Retirement Annuity Plans are paid gross. Contributions to personal pension schemes are paid net.

     1 mark

Appropriate personal pension schemes may receive contributions from a member's employer and also the DWP (formerly the DSS) by way of minimum contributions (age related rebates).

     1 mark

The maximum tax free cash sum from a retirement annuity is three times the residual pension.

     1 mark

The maximum tax free cash sum from a personal pension scheme is 25% of the fund excluding protected rights.

     1 mark

1 mark

Providers of retirement annuities are limited to insurance companies and friendly societies.

1 mark
Total 8 marks

Providers of personal pension schemes comprise the above and other institutions such as banks, building societies and unit trust companies.

1 mark

A5   Contributions by members receive full income tax relief. Contributions up to £3,600 gross per annum are paid without reference to income and even non-earners gain from the basic rate tax relief.

1 mark

Any employer contribution is allowable as a business expense.

1 mark

Employer contributions are not treated as benefit in kind in the hands of the member.

1 mark

The fund accumulated out of Personal Pension contributions grows free from tax on income and capital gains. (UK dividend tax credits cannot be reclaimed.)

1 mark

Up to 25% of the non-protected rights fund may be taken as a tax-free cash sum.

1 mark
Total 6 marks

Death benefits from personal pension plans may be paid under trust and therefore free of inheritance tax.

1 mark

A6   With an Individual Savings Account, the value of the ISA forms a part of the ISA holders estate.

1 mark

The ISA investment cannot be held in trust.

1 mark

With a PPP, the fund value is available and forms of a part of the deceased's estate.

1 mark

Usually the PPP is written under trust, in which case IHT can be avoided.

2 marks

Under a PPP set up before 6 April 2001, additional life cover may be purchased with premiums of up to 5% of net relevant earnings. For PPPs set up after 5 April 2001, the limit for life cover payments is 10% of the contributions made towards retirement benefits.

1 mark
Total 7 marks

This life cover may be also be written under trust, so avoiding IHT.

1 mark

A7   (a)   Employee contributions are set at 1.5% of pensionable pay.

1 mark

     AVCs may be used to buy added years or may be invested into separate money purchase-based arrangements.

1 mark

    (b)   The Scheme provides a pension of 1/80th of final salary for each year of membership.

3 marks

     The pension is inflation proofed to the Retail Prices Index plus a tax free lump sum of three time the pension benefit (accept 3/80ths of final salary for each year of service).

2 marks

    (c)   On death in service, the scheme pays a lump sum of two times salary plus a spouse's pension which is inflation linked.

Total 8 marks

1 mark

A8   Purchased Life Annuities may produce a higher level of income than an equivalent pension annuity.

2 marks

The PLA income is deemed to be composed of two elements a return of capital and an investment income (1). The capital element is not taxed (1).

1 mark

The investment element is taxed at 20%, which settles the liability for a basic rate tax payer.

1 mark
Total 5 marks

A Compulsory Purchase Pension is taxed as earned income on the whole amount.

1 mark

A9   It would be advantageous for the client to take the open market option.

The Retirement Annuity Plan will provide a tax free cash amount of three times the residual pension. $3 \times £7,000 = £21,000$.

The tax-free cash from a Personal Pension Plan is 25% of the fund value (1). Therefore the tax-free cash here would be £25,000 (1).

2 marks
Total 5 marks

A10 She may purchase a pension for herself with the fund value.

1 mark

She may continue to make withdrawals from the fund (1) until the earliest of her 75 birthday or when Brian would have been 75 (1).

2 marks

She may take the fund as a lump sum (1), which is subject to a 35% tax charge (1).

2 marks
Total 5 marks

A11 The employee is taxed on any contributions made by the employer as a benefit in kind.

1 mark

The employer will be allowed to offset any contributions against their taxable profits.

1 mark

The employee is not entitled to tax relief on any personal contributions.

1 mark

The fund itself will pay Income and Capital Gains Tax.

1 mark

Due to the fact that the fund has been taxed, a lump sum can be taken from the fund tax-free. However, any pension bought would be taxable.

1 mark
Total 5 marks

A12 Stephen may decide to continue with the FSAVC, in which case it would become attached to the new employer's Occupational Pension Scheme.

1 mark

Contributions may cease and the fund will become paid up.

1 mark

The whole fund value could be transferred to a Personal Pension. (The transfer would be subject to a Nil Cash Certificate preventing tax-free cash being paid on this part of the fund.)

1 mark

It is possible to transfer the fund to another FSAVC.

1 mark

The fund value may be transferred into the new pension scheme.

1 mark

It is possible to take the pension if the client is aged over 50.

1 mark
To be marked out of a total of five

A13 The benefits of a Personal Pension may be taken between ages 50 and 75.

1 mark

The member does not have to stop working to benefit from the pension fund.

1 mark

There are a number of 'special occupations', eg athletes, who may retire before age 50.

1 mark

Where the member has to stop work because of permanent incapacity, it is also possible to draw on the fund.

1 mark

Benefits are only payable on permanent incapacity, ie the member is unlikely to be able to return to work.

1 mark
Total 5 marks

A14 Age related rebates were introduced in the Act.

1 mark

The employer's contribution (flat rate) is supplemented by an age-related rebate from the DSS.

1 mark

If the member is single when the protected right pension is bought, the part of the fund that has accrued in respect of employment since 5 April 1997 does not have to be used to buy a spouse's annuity.

1 mark

In respect of the fund that has accrued from 6 April 1997, Limited Price Indexation based increases must take place.

1 mark

BPP PUBLISHING

Marking scheme

1 mark

The Act had a number of wide-ranging effects such as the requirement for Member-Nominated Trustees.

Total 5 marks

1 mark

A15 It is possible for Martin to delay purchasing the annuity and an income may be taken directly from the fund.

1 mark

Martin must purchase his annuity by the time he is aged 75.

1 mark

Actuarial certification of the income drawdown is required every three years.

2 marks

The income must be within 10% of that available from the available fund as certified by the scheme actuary.

Total 5 marks

A16 The two definitions are as follows.

2 marks

Basic pay in any 12 month period during the last five years plus the average of three or more years' fluctuating emoluments.

3 marks

Average of three or more consecutive years' pay ending no later than 10 years before retirement. Earnings may be indexed by RPI if they are more than 12 months before retirement. This is known as dynamisation.

Total 5 marks

1 mark

A17 The fund must be valued at regular intervals by an actuary to ensure that it has sufficient assets to meet its liabilities.

2 marks

Should the actuarial valuation discover that the scheme is underfunded ie the fund has assets which are worth 90% or less of its liabilities. The employer must ensure that the 90% level is achieved within 12 months.

1 mark

The current transitional arrangements mean that the employer has until 5 April 2003 to ensure that any serious underprovision is corrected.

1 mark
Total 5 marks

The full provisions of the Minimum Funding Requirement do not come into effect until 6 April 2007.

1 mark

A18 There are three methods used to deal with the pension fund value on divorce: earmarking, balancing or 'off-setting' and pension sharing.

Earmarking involves part of the fund being paid to Dora at a later date.

1 mark
1 mark
Total 5 marks

Balancing or off-setting involves taking the value of the fund into account when deciding on the settlement with the estranged partner.

1 mark

Pension sharing is possible where divorce proceedings started on or after 1 December 2000. The rights of each spouse are separated at the time of the divorce. The member's benefits are reduced, to provide pension rights for the ex-spouse, under her control.

1 mark

Balancing or *pension sharing* have the advantage that a clean break may be achieved.

2 marks

A19 The SSAS can borrow 45% of the fund (1) which is £250,000 × 45% = £112,500 (1).

2 marks

In addition three times ordinary annual contributions (1) 3 × £65,000 = 195,000 (1).

1 mark

The total amount that may be borrowed by the scheme is £307,500.

Total 5 marks

A20 (a) The SSAS is limited on the amount it may borrow to finance the property purchase. The amount borrowed may be no more than 45% of the fund value plus three times ordinary annual contributions.

2 marks

2 marks

A SIPP borrowing for purposes of property purchase or development is, from 6 April 2001, restricted to a maximum of 75% of the purchase price or cost of development respectively. Any such loan must be secured on the property and must be repaid if the property is sold.

(b) A SSAS may only purchase a property, which has a residential element, where the residential element is in connection with the employment of the individual, for example a caretaker. The person living in the property may not be connected with a member of the scheme.

Marking scheme

2 marks

SIPPs may not invest in residential property, except as follows:

2 marks

(i) Residential property occupied, or to be occupied, by an employee, even if a member of the SIPP, provided that the employee is not connected to the employer and is required as a condition of his employment to occupy the property (eg a caretaker's flat).

(ii) Residential property occupied, or to be occupied, by someone who is not a member of the SIPP and is not connected with a member, where the occupation of the residential property is in connection with the occupation of business premises under the scheme (again an example is a caretaker's flat).

(c) A SSAS is prohibited from jointly owning property unless they have the right to sell the property at any time without the agreement of the co-owner.

1 mark

SIPPs may own property in joint names. It is common for partners to combine funds to buy commercial property.

1 mark
Total 10 marks

A21 Those employees who remain subject to income tax in the UK will have the right to continue accruing benefits.

2 marks

Crown employees working abroad, such as members of the armed forces.

1 mark

Where the employee is stationed overseas but expects to return to the UK within 10 years. The UK employers must pay the contributions into the scheme for the member and then reclaim them from the employer in the overseas location.

2 marks
Total 5 marks

A22 (a) The benefits from the NHS scheme are based on an accrual rate of $1/80^{th}$ for each year of service.

1 mark

$35 \times 1/80^{th} \times £22,000 = £9,625$

1 mark

(b) Death in service lump sum would be two times salary or £42,000. 44000

1 mark
Total 3 marks

A23 (a) The maximum that may be paid for life cover is 10% of the amount paid for retirement benefits. Sandy's maximum life cover would be the amount that this could purchase from an insurance company.

1 mark

(b) The maximum contribution that Sandy may make in the current year, making use of carry back relief, would be as follows.

2000/01   20% × £25,000 = £5,000

2 marks

2001/02   20% × £30,800 = £6,160, of which one-eleventh (£560) could provide life cover.

2 marks

The maximum contribution into the plan is £5,000 + £6,160 − £560 = £10,600.

2 marks

The carry back election must be made by the date of the contribution and not later than 31 January 2002.

Total 7 marks

A24 (a) The election to contract out could be effective from April 2000 or April 2001.

2 marks

(b) There are several circumstances in which the DWP (formerly the DSS) would cease to make payments into the Appropriate Personal Pension, as follows.

• If Stephen becomes a member of an occupational scheme that is contracted out — 1 mark
• If Stephen earns less than the lower earnings limit in the tax year — 1 mark
• If Stephen completes APP2, contracting back into SERPS — 1 mark
• If Stephen decides to become self-employed — 1 mark
• If Stephen goes to work outside the UK — 1 mark

Total 7 marks

BPP PUBLISHING

Exam answer bank

A25 The reasons why Brian may wish to sacrifice salary in order to increase his pension contribution are as follows.

1 mark
- He currently contributes only 6% of his salary into the scheme. Therefore it is unlikely that he will achieve anywhere near Inland Revenue maximum benefits.

1 mark
- By sacrificing, salary he is not restricted to the 15% of remuneration that limits employee contributions.

1 mark
1 mark
- There is a saving in National Insurance Contributions for the employer who is ostensibly making the contribution on behalf of the employee. It is possible that the employer may contribute the saving in National Insurance Contributions into the scheme as additional pension contributions.

Total 4 marks

A26 There are a number of ways in which an individual may receive credit for National Insurance without making compulsory contributions, as follows.

1 mark
- The DWP will credit the contribution history of individuals who are claiming a number of benefits such as unemployment maternity benefits sickness benefits.

1 mark
- Paying voluntary contributions (Class 3 contributions).

1 mark
- If the individual is staying on at school or education between 16 and 18.

1 mark
- Where the individual is a male aged over 60 and under 65 years of age.

Total 4 marks

2 marks
A27 There is a direct relationship between gilt yields and annuity rates. So if the gilt yield fell the annuity rate would follow suit.

2 marks
This means that a larger fund will be required to provide the same level of income at retirement because the annuity has become more expensive.

1 mark
Critical yield from the transfer analysis will tend to increase.

Total 5 marks

A28 (a) The maximum contribution that Sally could make to her personal pension would be

3 marks
$17.5\% \times £95,400$ (Earnings cap) $= £16,695$.

1 mark
(b) Sally has a special occupation approved by the Inland Revenue. As she is an athlete she can retire at age 35.

1 mark
(c) The latest that she can defer taking her pension benefits is age 75.

Total 5 marks

A29 (a) The factors that normally influence the level of income are the age of the individual concerned, the gender of the individual and the gilt yield as published in the FT on the

3 marks
15th of the month.

(b) The maximum withdrawal that Peter will be entitled to is:

1 mark
$85 \times £250 = £21,250$

1 mark
The minimum entitlement will be:

$£21,250 \times 35\% = £7,437.50$

1 mark
(c) The level of income from the plan must be reassessed every three years.

Total 6 marks

1 mark
A30 (a) 5 March 1953: between 60 and 65.

1 mark
(b) 7 January 1958: 65.

1 mark
(c) 19 October 1949: 60.

1 mark
(d) 25 March 1955: between 60 and 65.

Total 4 marks

Marking scheme

A31 (a) Where there is a surviving spouse or other dependant at the time of death, the lump sum payment is limited to 25% of the fund.

1 mark

The fund value after commutation must be used to buy a spouse's annuity.

1 mark

The protected rights fund must be used to buy a survivor's annuity which escalates at a prescribed rate.

1 mark

(b) In the event that there is no surviving spouse or other dependent at the date of death, the treatment of the fund is very straightforward. It may be paid entirely as a lump sum to the specified beneficiaries.

2 marks

Total 5 marks

A32 (a) A contribution to a Personal Pension Plan by an employer is always paid gross to the scheme and the tax credit is reclaimed as an allowable expense against taxable profits.

2 marks

The contribution made by the employer into the employee's pension fund would not be treated as a benefit in kind.

1 mark

It is not possible for the employer to carry back contributions.

1 mark

(b) If a payment is made by an employer into a Retirement Annuity Plan, it is treated as if the employer has paid additional salary to the employee so the employee is taxed on the benefit but receives relief on the contribution.

2 marks

The employer will pay the premium gross. The tax relief is then reclaimed by the employee.

1 mark

Total 7 marks

A33 (a) The refund that would be paid by the FSAVC scheme would be:

£7,000 × 68% (tax is charged at 32%) = £4,760

2 marks

(b) She will have to pay additional tax.

1 mark

She has paid £2,240.

This is deemed to have met the liability to basic rate tax. Therefore the £4,676 must be grossed up by $^{100}/_{78}$ which will give:

$£4,760 \times {}^{100}/_{78} = £6,102.56$

1 mark

The difference between the basic rate of 22% and the higher rate of 40% is 18%.

1 mark

$£6,102.56 \times 18\% = £1,098.46$

The total tax paid is £2,240 + £1,098.46 = £3,338.46 or 47.69%.

1 mark

Total 6 marks

A34 There are a number of schemes that can be used to preserve the accrued benefits from a contracted-out final salary scheme upon winding up.

(i) Transfer to a Personal Pension Plan

1 mark

(ii) Transfer to a Section 32 buy out bond

1 mark

(iii) Transfer to another occupational pension scheme

1 mark

(iv) Transfer to a deferred annuity contract

1 mark

Total 4 marks

A35 (a) The transfer club is an arrangement between public sector schemes to credit employees transferring between the members of the club with equal service in terms of the pension history.

2marks

(b) The employee will wish to take advantage of the transfer club as it will ensure that the member will continue to enjoy continuity of pension rights. Where the transfer value is low, the receiving scheme will boost the pension so that an equivalent number of pensionable years are credited to the member.

3 marks

Total 5 marks

BPP
PUBLISHING

SECTION B ANSWERS

2 marks	B1	(a)	A Small Self Administered Scheme with the scheme owning the property.

2 marks — A Small Self Administered Scheme with a loan back to the employer who makes the purchase and owns the property.

2 marks — A Self Invested Personal Pension with the scheme owning the property.

2 marks — A Funded Unapproved Retirement Benefit Scheme.

2 marks
Total 10 marks — An Executive Pension Scheme with a loan back to the company with the company then purchasing the property.

(b)   Funds could be transferred to a SIPP for each of the individuals to enable the property purchase jointly.

2 marks

2 marks — Funds could be transferred to a SSAS to enable the property purchase.

2 marks — However transfer penalties would need to be analysed carefully,

2 marks — as would the loss of benefits from the final salary scheme.

2 marks — Neither the SSAS nor the SIPP could accept the GMP liability.

2 marks
Total 12 marks — Consider the amount that may be invested into a SSAS as compared to the total amounts that may be invested into SIPPS, particularly given the 1996 funding requirement.

(c)   *SSAS*

1 mark — The scheme may invest in commercial property.

2 marks — Residential property is allowed if occupied by an employee who is not connected with his or her employer and who is required as a condition of employment to occupy the property.

2 marks — The scheme trustees cannot buy or sell any investment from or to a member of the scheme or any other connected individual other than the principal employer.

2 marks — A professional valuation is required.

2 marks — Property purchase must be reported to Inland Revenue within 90 days.

1 mark — ~~Care needs to be taken if the member is within 90 days.~~

1 mark — Care needs to be taken if the member is within 10 years of NRD.

SIPP

2 marks — The SIPP may invest in commercial property.

1 mark — Residential property is permitted if occupied, or to be occupied, by an employee, even if a member of the SIPP, provided that the employee is not connected to the employer and is required as a condition of his employment to occupy the property (eg a caretaker's flat).

1 mark — Residential property is also permitted if occupied, or to be occupied, by someone who is not a member of the SIPP and is not connected with a member, where the occupation of the residential business is in connection with the occupation of business premises under the scheme (again an example is a caretaker's flat).

2 marks — From 6 April 2001, borrowing for property purchase is limited to 75% of the purchase price.

2 marks — Any such loan must be secured on the property and must be repaid if the property is sold.

Generally a lender will want to see that the loan can be serviced from rental income and ongoing contributions to the SIPP.

2 marks

A professional valuation will be required.

2 marks

The SIPP cannot buy or sell any investment from or to a member of the scheme or any other connected individual.

2 marks

The lease to the employer or other party should be on commercial terms.

2 marks

Total 27 marks

(d) Funding levels are certified by an actuary as part of a funding review of the scheme, taking into account members' remuneration levels and existing values.

2 marks

The funding review in effect sets maximum contribution levels which must be reviewed every three years.

2 mark

No check on funding is required if contributions do not exceed 17.5% of the member's remuneration or for schemes established prior to 31 March 1998.

3 marks

Existing assets will be valued at market value.

2 marks

Special contributions will have to be actuarially justified in accordance with Inland Revenue requirements.

2 marks

If justified, they will get tax relief with no spread rules applying.

1 mark

However, relief will be spread if special contribution exceeds £500,000.

2 marks

Relief may be spread over a maximum of four years.

2 marks

The calculation basis is broadly the same as post-Sept 1994 funding rules for EPPs and will lead to a funding rate as a maximum percentage of salary.

2 marks

Factors to be taken into account are:

Rate of investment return	8.5%
Rate of salary growth	6.9%
Rate of pension escalation	5.3%
Price inflation	5.3%

1 mark

1 mark

1 mark

1 mark

The contribution rate to be reassessed very three years or on the payment of a special contribution with a new three year period then starting.

4 marks

Total 26 marks

B2 Assume that Kevin wants to retire ten years before his scheme's Normal Retirement Date and that he has a moderate risk profile.

(a) (i) The deferred pension from the first employer's scheme is $6/60 \times £20,000 = £2,000$.

1 mark

The deferred pension from the second employer's scheme is $9/60 \times £39,000 = £5,500$.

1 mark

(ii) GMP must be revalued to NRD for each complete tax year to NRD.

2 marks

The revaluation rate is 7.5% because the member left in September 1990

1 marks

The excess over the GMP must also be revalued.

1 marks

Only the part of the excess over the GMP fund that has accrued from 1 January 1985 will be revalued.

2 marks

The pre-1 January 1985 excess over GMP benefits may not receive revaluation.

2 marks

The excess over the GMP on the post-31 December 1984 benefits will be revalued for each year to NRD at 5% per annum or RPI if less.

2 marks

BPP
PUBLISHING

(iii)   The pension from the second employer's scheme is increased by Retail Prices Index in deferment.

(b)   (i)   The scheme may offer the following.

1 mark
1 mark
1 mark

    (1)   Added years
    (2)   Fixed benefits
    (3)   Money purchase

(ii)   *Added years*

1 mark for
each point

Advantages	Disadvantages
Pension is certain as it is guaranteed as a fraction of final salary	They are not good value for frequent job changers
Added years are particularly good value for those who expect rapid promotion in the company	If added years are transferred 'like for like' benefits are not normally given

Fixed benefits

Advantages	Disadvantages
Guaranteed amount of pension paid on retirement	Fixed amount could be eroded by inflation
Good if inflation is lower than the inflation figure used to calculate the revalued pension	Pension is likely to represent a reducing proportion of earnings

Money purchase

Advantages	Disadvantages
Greater flexibility at retirement	Loses guarantees of a fixed pension offered by a final salary scheme
Investment performance could be better than expected	There is a double risk in that investment performance could be poor and also that annuity rates are low when he wants to buy his annuity

Total 15 marks

2 marks

(c)   *Inland Revenue Maximum Pensions for each scheme*

First scheme

Kevin joined as a pre-87 member of the scheme. Therefore no earnings cap would apply.

1 mark

He has 9 years actual service out of a potential of 39 years.

3 marks

Maximum pension is therefore $(9/39 \times 2/3) \times £20,000 = £3,077$.

3 marks

Maximum lump sum is $(9/39 \times 3/2) \times £20,000 = £6,923$.

Second scheme

1 mark

Kevin joined as a post-89 member of the scheme.

3 marks

Maximum pension under this scheme would be $9/30 \times £51,500 = £15,450$.

3 marks

Maximum tax-free cash is greater of $27/80 \times £51,500$ and $2.25 \times$ actual pension before commutation.

2 marks

Total 18 marks

Pension and retained benefits are not allowed to exceed 2/3 of final remuneration.

(d) (i) The first employers scheme was contracted out of SERPS a widow's GMP must be provided. *Marking scheme*
2 marks

The remaining fund can be paid as a lump sum of up to four times remuneration.   2 marks

(ii) 25% of the total fund value may be taken as a lump sum.   2 marks

Whilst protected rights are included for calculating the 25%, the protected rights fund itself may not be commuted for cash.   1 mark

The protected rights fund must buy a widow's pension as Sally is a qualifying spouse.   2 marks

(iii) This scheme is contracted-in so a lump sum of four times final remuneration less retained benefits could be paid.   2 marks

This could amount to the whole fund.   1 mark

(iv) A lump sum of 25% of the fund value may be taken and the remainder of the fund used to buy a widow's pension.   3 marks
Total 15 marks

(e) The factors you would use to decide between a S32 plan and a personal pension   1 mark per point made

Personal Pension Plan	*Section 32*
Protected rights can only be taken from age 60	GMP could be taken when Kevin wants to retire at age 55, providing he has sufficient funds to pay at least revalued GMP at age 65
A personal pension offers greater choice of fund	As GMP is guaranteed the insurer generally requires investment in 'With Profits' funds to cover his liability
There is no risk of over-funding a Personal Pension Plan and there are many ways benefits may be taken	Death benefits lump sums are higher than under a Personal Pension Plan
Personal Pension Plan can not be transferred to a Section 32	Tax-free cash is likely to be higher under a s 32
Personal Pension Plan may accept a transfer-in	Possible to over-fund a s 32 plan especially if Kevin changes his mind and wants at age 65
Personal Pension Plan can allow contributions in the future	S 32 can be transferred to a Personal Pension Plan
	S 32 cannot allow future contributions

Total 13 marks

B3 (a) (i) • Harry had been in the scheme for 17 years
    • Deferred pension was 17/60ths of £110,000   1 mark
    • That is £31,166.67 pa   1 mark

(ii) The Guaranteed Minimum Pension accrued to 5 April 1997 will be revalued for each complete tax year between December 2001 and State Pension Age.   1 mark   1 mark

The GMP will at the very least keep its earnings-based value but if the scheme uses fixed rate revaluation and if earnings inflation over the period is less than 6.25% pa, the GMP will do more than maintain its earnings based value.   1 mark   2 marks

Where the scheme uses fixed or limited rate revaluation, some degree of this earnings based value protection on the GMP may come from the State.   1 mark   2 marks

The excess benefit over the GMP that, at the very least, has accrued since 1 January 1985 must be increased in line with the Retail Prices Index to a maximum of 5% pa (reference to LPI *not* acceptable) between December 2001 and normal retirement date.   1 mark   1 mark   1 mark
Total 15 marks

BPP PUBLISHING

1 mark

(b) • Calculate Harry's preserved pension at December 2001

1 mark

1 mark   • Revalue Harry's preserved pension to normal retirement age,
using assumed RPI inflation on the excess over the GMP

1 mark   and if the scheme uses full or limited revaluation of the GMP

1 mark   taking account of assumed earnings inflation over the period to State Pension
Age

1 mark

1 mark   • Capitalise the revalued benefits to a lump sum at normal retirement age
based on assumed annuity rates.

1 mark   Allowance made for any discretionary increases in pension benefits to be taken

1 mark   account of where the assumption will be based on recent history of discretionary
increases.

1 mark

1 mark   • Discount back the capitalised sum to today's value using an assumed investment
growth rate.

Total 11 marks

1 mark   (c) • Tax free cash certification applies

1 mark   as Harry would be over age 45 at the time of any such transfer.

1 mark

1 mark   • And because Harry was a controlling (20%) director

1 mark   in the ten years before leaving the scheme

1 mark   and Harry had remuneration in excess of the earnings cap

1 mark   in the last ten years.

1 mark

1 mark   • Harry's maximum tax-free cash sum is restricted to 25%

1 mark   of the non-protected rights fund,

1 mark   or the certified tax-free cash sum

1 mark   increased from December 2001

1 mark   to the date benefits are taken

1 mark   by the Index of Retail Prices.

• The tax free cash sum as a part of the non-protected rights benefits is available

Total 13 marks   at any time after age 50.

2 marks   (d) • The transfer to the personal pension cannot proceed
if the transfer value is excessive.

1 mark   • This arises because any such transfer is subject to a general/overfunding
certificate

1 mark   ie a GN11 test will be necessary.

• This is an actuarial test to ensure that Harry does not benefit from the lack of

2 marks   maximum benefit restrictions in a personal pension

1 mark   by taking a transfer value that is excessive in relation to maximum benefit limits.

• The need for this test is because Harry was a controlling (20%) director in the

1 mark   ten years before leaving the scheme

2 marks   and Harry had remuneration in excess of the earnings cap.

1 mark   • Non-protected rights benefits may not be taken before age 50

1 mark   and a pension annuity from the non-protected rights fund must be secured by
age 75.

1 mark   • Protected rights benefits may not be taken before age 60

1 mark   and a pension annuity from the protected rights fund must be secured by age 75.

- On death before benefits are taken, the maximum lump sum is 25% of the total fund which is taken from the non-protected rights fund.

- The remaining fund is used to provide pension benefits for any qualifying spouse or other dependant subject to the usual restrictions applicable to protected rights on escalation.

- Otherwise the whole fund may be paid in lump sum form.

(e)
- On transfer to a Section 32 plan, the revalued GMP must be in place at State Pension Age.

- If benefits are taken before State pension age, the benefit secured must cover the revalued GMP.

- The tax free cash sum is restricted to the Inland Revenue maximum
  at the date of leaving
  revalued by RPI to the date benefits are taken.

- The pension value of the overall benefits taken must not exceed Inland Revenue maximum limits as at the date of leaving
  again revalued by RPI.

- Otherwise the Section 32 plan becomes overfunded
  and the member may not benefit from the excess
  which will be returned to First Millennium Packaging Ltd
  or if they no longer exist will be retained by the receiving life office.

- The post 5 April 1997 benefit must escalate in line with Limited price indexation
  that is at RPI capped to maximum of 5% pa.

- The pre 5 April 1997 GMP must escalate in line with RPI
  the first 3% pa of such escalation on the post 5 April 1988 GMP coming from the Section 32 plan.

- On death before benefits are taken the maximum lump sum is four times remuneration at the date of leaving service
  after providing for any spouse's GMP.

- The remaining fund is used to provide pension benefits for any spouse or other dependant within Inland Revenue limits.

B4 (a) (i)
- Member nominated trustees are required unless acceptable alternative arrangements were put forward by the employer.

- Any compensation scheme levy payments are required.

- This means that the post 5 April 1997 fund must provide for pensions that increase in payment at 5% pa or RPI if less.

- The Occupational Pensions Regulatory Authority oversees the running of all such schemes with a levy on the scheme.

- The trustees of the scheme must ensure that proper procedures exist to resolve disputes about the scheme and that these procedures are notified to the members.

Marking scheme
1 mark
1 mark
1 mark
1 mark
1 mark
Total 19 marks
1 mark

1 mark

1 mark

1 mark

1 mark

1 mark

1 mark

1 mark
1 mark
1 mark

1 mark

1 mark

1 mark

1 mark

1 mark

1 mark

1 mark

Total 17 marks

1 mark
1 mark

2 marks

1 mark

1 mark
1 mark
1 mark
1 mark
1 mark
1 mark

Marking scheme 1 mark	• It is a civil offence not to keep a separate trustees' bank account and proper records of all transactions and of trustees' meetings are required.
2 marks	• It is a criminal offence for the employer to deduct employee contributions and then not to forward them to the scheme within the prescribed time limits.
1 mark 1 mark	• The link to SERPS via a notional GMP no longer applies so the State no longer bears any responsibility in relation to the inflation-proofing of benefits.
1 mark	• Age-related rebates are payable by the National Insurance Contributions Office (NICO) to the scheme in addition to redirected NICs.

(ii)
- The post 5 April 1997 protected rights fund is subject to own status rather than uni-status annuity rates.

1 mark

- This means that if single when the protected rights benefits are taken, the fund need not provide for a 50% spouse's pension.

1 mark
1 mark

- When used by members to contract out, age-related rebates apply.

1 mark

- The post 5 April 1997 protected rights fund must provide for pensions that increase in payment at 5% pa or RPI if less.

Total 21 marks

(b)
- The scheme would need to satisfy a test of quality.

1 mark

- This is set by benchmarking to a reference scheme.

1 mark

Benefits from the scheme for males and females must be payable by age 65.

1 mark

- Pension benefits must be at least 1/80th of 90%

1 mark

of earnings above the lower earnings limit and below the upper earnings limit

1 mark

for each year of scheme membership to a maximum of 40 years.

1 mark

- Pensions must increase in payment by at least the increase in RPI or 5%.

2 marks

- The scheme must provide for a minimum of a 50% spouse's pension.

1 mark

- The test must be met in respect of at least 90% of the membership.

1 mark

- The test is satisfied by certification by the scheme actuary generally every three years that the reference scheme requirements are being met.

2 marks

Total 12 marks

(c) (i)
1 mark
1 mark
1 mark
- A history of Class 1 and/or Class 2 NI contributions over 90% of John's working life

1 mark
- Working life – 49 years

(ii)
- Form BR19 is completed and forwarded to the Benefits Agency.

1 mark
- The pension estimate will show the basic State pension.

1 mark
- The pension estimate will show any SERPS.

1 mark
- The pension estimate will show any Graduated Pension.

1 mark
- The pension estimate will show the voluntary Class 3 NICs that may be paid to 'top up' any basic state pension shortfall.

1 mark

Total 9 marks

(d) (i)
- With the old scheme, the scheme was contracted out, so all members of the scheme were contracted out — 1 mark

- With a GPP, contracting out is the decision of the member — 1 mark

- The ex-scheme members who contract out through personal pensions will pay full rate NICs — 1 mark

- Age-related rebates will be paid by the NICO to the contracted-out personal pension after the end of each tax year. — 1 mark

- Under the old scheme, reduced rate NICs were paid, with the reduction being redirected to the members' protected rights fund. — 1 mark

- Age related additions were paid direct by the NICO. — 1 mark

(ii)
- If the scheme is left in paid-up form, then the benefits may be left where they are. — 1 mark

- A transfer could be taken to any scheme of a new employer if the member leaves the company. — 1 mark

- A transfer could be taken to a personal pension plan of the member's choice. — 1 mark

- A transfer could be taken to the GPP if the member has joined it. — 1 mark

- A transfer could be taken to a Section 32 plan. — 1 mark

- It may be possible for the plan benefit to be assigned to an individual policy. — 1 mark

(iii)
- The company could decide to implement no additional arrangements, leaving the members to make their own arrangements — 1 mark

- The company could offer the individual's membership of the existing GPP on the same matched contribution basis. — 1 mark

- The company could offer the individual's membership of the existing GPP on different terms for example with a higher level of employer contribution. — 2 marks

- The company could offer the individuals membership of a separate GPP — 1 mark

- The company could offer to pay contributions to a personal pension of the members choice. — 1 mark

Total 18 marks

(e)
- Harriet could leave her fund to accumulate within the scheme. — 1 mark

- The fund will continue to accumulate until Harriet takes benefits. — 1 mark

- A transfer value may be taken to any occupational scheme of a new employer — 1 mark

- Or to another personal pension of Harriet's choice. — 1 mark

- If Harriet joins a new employer that has no occupational scheme then they may continue paying contributions to her personal pension account. — 1 mark

- These contributions may simply be a continuation of the contributions she was making, may include the employer's contributions, or may be any other amount within permissible limits — 1 mark

- If Harriet becomes self-employed, she may continue making personal pension contributions within the maximum permissible percentage of net relevant earnings. — 1 mark

- Contributions will be paid net of basic rate tax, with higher rate tax being reclaimable. — 1 mark

Total 9 marks

(f)
- Where the employee is subject to the earnings cap. — 1 mark

BPP PUBLISHING

Marking scheme

- Where benefits over and above the maximum allowable elsewhere are to be provided through a FURBS having first maximised the use of approved arrangements

2 marks

- To retain/recruit high quality staff

1 mark

- To provide death benefits over the four times capped earnings limit.

2 marks

Total 6 marks

B5   (a)   UK pension provision is in three tiers:

1 mark

- Basic state pension
  a subsistence level of income
  requiring a satisfactory history of payments to or credits to the National Insurance system.

1 mark

1 mark

- SERPS:
  an earnings related second tier pension introduced in 1978
  where the benefits have been scaled down due to cost
  or alternatives to it by contracting out.

1 mark

1 mark

1 mark

1 mark

- Additional private provision or through an employer's scheme

1 mark

- The employees of Boyle and Bubble Ltd are contributing to the Basic state pension if they earn more than the lower earnings limit - there is no choice.

1 mark

1 mark

1 mark

1 mark

- The employees of Boyle and Bubble Ltd are in SERPs by default unless they make arrangements to contract out personally.

1 mark

- They may choose to contract out of SERPs via an appropriate personal pension.

1 mark

- If they are in the Boyle and Bubble Ltd money purchase scheme, this will be on a rebate only basis
  and could be through a contracted out FSAVC.

1 mark

1 mark

- The employees of Boyle and Bubble Ltd may choose to join the Boyle and Bubble Ltd money purchase scheme
  once they satisfy the eligibility conditions
  or they may choose not to join it.

1 mark

1 mark

1 mark

- Those who are in it may leave the scheme at any time.

1 mark

- Those not in the Boyle and Bubble Ltd money purchase scheme may effect a personal pension and pay into it personally.

1 mark

- Those not in the Boyle and Bubble Ltd money purchase scheme may decide to make no additional pension provision and rely wholly on the state.

1 mark

- Those in the Boyle and Bubble Ltd money purchase scheme may pay AVCs to the scheme to top up their benefits, or pay up to £3,600 pa gross into a personal pension if not controlling directors since 6 April 2001 and if earnings below £30,000 in 2000/01.

1 mark

1 mark

- Those in the Boyle and Bubble Ltd money purchase scheme may pay FSAVCs to a provider of their choice to top up their benefits
  and may pay in scheme AVCs in addition within the allowable contribution limits.

1 mark

Total 25 marks

(b) • The basic state pension is intended to remain and to keep its value in line with prices.

    • SERPS is to be abolished and replaced by the State Second Pension (S2P). Although initially retaining the earnings related characteristics of SERPS, the S2P will in time become a flat rate benefit.

    • The proposals assume that those earning up to about £9,000 pa will get all of their pension provided by the State because this group cannot afford a pension of their own.

    • Over their working life, those earning up to about £9,000 pa and over the lower earnings limit will accrue the State Second Pension based on a maximum of 40% of middle band earnings but assuming they have earnings of £9,000 pa.

    • This is twice the level of SERPS at the £9,000 pa level of earnings.

    • Those earning over £9,000 pa and up to about £18,500 pa will earn the S2P but based on a maximum of 10% of earnings over £9,000. At the margin, this is less than SERPS accrual.

    • Those earning more than about £18,500 pa will accrue the S2P based on a maximum of 20% of earnings over £18,500 and up to the upper earning limit
      On the margin this is the same as SERPS accrual.

    • At £18,500 pa, SERPS and the S2P provide about the same benefit – at least initially.

    • When stakeholder pensions have become well established the S2P is to become a flat rate scheme based on the £9,000 pa level of earnings.

2 marks

1 mark
1 mark
1 mark
1 mark
1 mark
1 mark
1 mark

1 mark
1 mark
1 mark

1 mark

1 mark
1 mark

2 marks

1 mark

1 mark

3 marks

Total 22 marks

(c) • Those who earn under about £18,500 pa will do better from the state than they do now and may also join the money purchase scheme if it continues to operate, or any designated stakeholder pension scheme.

    • Anyone earning less than £9,000 pa will most likely be well served by the S2P with any additional provision through any designated stakeholder pension scheme.

    • Provision of access to a designated stakeholder pension scheme is obligatory from 8 October 2001 unless Boyle and Bubble Ltd offers membership of an occupational pension scheme that is 'suitable'.

    • This scheme could be suitable because the scheme meets stakeholder standards and can be designated as a stakeholder scheme or because of the level of employer contribution.

    • The existing scheme could be suitable, subject to any necessary modification.

    • The investment facilities may also need to be widened as the current with profits concept may not be suitable for a stakeholder scheme.

    • For those who are not in the existing money purchase scheme, it will be necessary to offer access to a stakeholder pension scheme.

    • Boyle and Bubble Ltd would need to choose the designated stakeholder pension scheme.

    • Boyle and Bubble Ltd will be required to consult the workforce on the choice of the nominated scheme.

    • Boyle and Bubble Ltd will have to collect contributions and send them to the designated stakeholder scheme.

2 marks

2 marks

2 marks

1 mark
1 mark

1 mark

2 marks

1 mark

1 mark
1 mark

1 mark

2 marks

Marking scheme

There is no obligation on Boyle and Bubble Ltd to contribute.

1 mark

- Members could use the stakeholder scheme to contract out and the receive state scheme rebates.

1 mark

Those using personal pensions for contracting out could continue to do so or could use the stakeholder scheme instead.

2 marks

1 mark

- Contracting out is likely to be most beneficial for those earning over £9,000 pa.

2 marks

- Boyle and Bubble Ltd may decide not to continue with the existing scheme at all but just to offer access to a stakeholder scheme and may continue to contribute for some employees.

2 marks

- Boyle and Bubble Ltd may decide to set up a grouped personal pension scheme that is stakeholder pension compliant.

2 marks

- Under the new 2001/02 rules, £3,600 gross pa may be contributed to stakeholder or other personal pension schemes.

Total 28 marks

SECTION C ANSWERS

C1   (a)   Geoff joined the scheme on 1 March 1983.

On leaving he had 11 complete years of membership.

So his deferred pension was 11/45ths of £54,000, ie £13,200 pa.

This will be increased at 5% pa or RPI if less until age 60.

LPI applies to 2/45 of £54,000, ie £2,400 pa.

This element of the deferred pension will not only be increased at 5% pa or RPI if less until age 60 but will similarly increase in payment, as will the associated spouse's pension.

There is a 50% spouse's pension at the date of leaving of £6,600 pa.

(b)   The critical yield is the growth required from the transfer value to match the scheme benefits at the scheme retirement date.

Achievement of a higher yield than 7.8% in either plan will give greater benefits based on the assumptions made in the analysis.

Achievement of a lower yield than 7.8% in either plan will give lower benefits based on the assumptions made in the analysis.

The critical yield appears to be low and may therefore favour the taking of a transfer value.

(c)   Taking the preserved pension will need the trustees consent if benefits are required earlier than age 60.

The scheme benefits will be substantially reduced to take account of it being taken 10 years early.

The effect of this should be quantified.

The critical yield may then be recalculated to the intended date at which benefits will be taken.

This will determine whether it remains the case that the transfer represents good value for money.

If the trustees of the scheme do not generally allow benefits to be taken early then Geoff may wish to take the transfer value anyway.

(d)   Geoff may wish to use a phased retirement facility.

By having the personal pension split into a large number of segments, he can vest as many segments as he wishes each year to meet overall income requirements.

Income will be represented by tax free cash from the vested segments and the income arising from the segments being cashed in as well as the cumulative income from the annuity arising from the earlier vesting of segments.

Annuity must be purchased from any uncashed segments by the age of 75.

Alternatively or in addition Geoff could use income drawdown facility.

Any tax free cash has to be taken at outset.

Income is drawn from remaining fund at up to that calculated by reference to tables issued by the Government actuary.

Minimum permitted income withdrawal is at 35% of this maximum figure.

Marking scheme
1 mark

Geoff may vary income each year within these limits and so meet his income requirement.

1 mark

Undrawn fund must be used to purchased an annuity by the age of 75.

Total 13 marks

1 mark
C2   (a)   Personal Pension Plan

1 mark
Occupational scheme ie Executive Pension Plan

1 mark
Funded Unapproved Retirement Benefits Scheme

1 mark
Unfunded Unapproved Retirement Benefits Scheme

Total 4 marks

		Personal Pension	Approved Occupational Pension	Unfunded Unapproved Scheme	Funded Unapproved Scheme
(b)	Contributions — Employee	Tax deductible up to contribution limits (1) — Not taxed as a benefit in kind (1)	Income Tax deductible up to 15% of total pay 1 Not taxed as a benefit in kind (1)	N/A	No reliefs (1) — Taxed on employee: counts a benefit in kind (1)
	Employer	Tax deductible as a business expense up to contribution limits (1)	Tax deductible as a business expense (1) — But possible spread (1)	N/A	Tax deductible – no spreading (1) — NICs payable (1)
(c)	Benefits — Pensions	Taxable no limits (1)	Taxable max. 2/3rds × (capped) Final Remuneration (1) — Including retained benefits (1)	Taxable – no limit	Taxable – no limit (1)
	Lump Sum	Tax free up 25% on fund (1) — Excluding protected Rights (1)	Tax free — Max 1.5 × (capped) Final Remuneration (1) — Including retained benefits (1)	Taxable – no limit	Tax free – no limit (1)
(d)	Investments – tax treatment	Tax free income and capital gains (2) (not dividend income)	Tax free income and capital gains (2) (not dividend income)	N/A (an unfunded promise to no investments held)	Income Taxed at basic rate (1) — Gains 34%
(e)	Security	Assets held on trust by provider (2)	Assets held under irrevocable trusts (2)	No assets	Assets held in trust (2)

BPP PUBLISHING

C3   (a)   The IR SPSS (formerly PSO) rules relating to borrowing are as follows.

1 mark

- The ordinary annual contribution of the employer multiplied by three.

2 marks

- Three times the annual member contributions, where member contributions are made as a condition of membership.

1 mark

- 45% of the market value of scheme investments.

4 marks

- Ordinary annual contribution means the average of employer contributions paid in the last three accounting periods of the SSAS, or averaged over a shorter period if the scheme has been established for less than three years at the time of any borrowing.

5 marks

- If some part of the scheme assets has become 'earmarked' for a retired member where use is being made of the facility to draw income directly from the fund with deferral of the pension purchase, then that part of the fund is not used towards the 45% limit on the scheme's investments.

1 mark

- The average contribution from the employer is £55,000.

1 mark

- Three times the employer average contribution is £165,000.

1 mark

- 45% of the fund value of £330,000 is £148,500.

1 mark
Total 17 marks

- The total permitted borrowing is £148,500 + £165,000 = £313,500.

1 mark

(b)
- The scheme owns the property and rents it to the company.

1 mark

- The company must pay a market rent for the property.

1 mark

- The rent paid may be set off against the taxable profits of the company.

2 marks

- The rent is received by the trustees of the scheme and is completely free of any tax.

2 marks

- Should the value of the property increase and the scheme decide to sell it, there would be no Capital Gains Tax to pay on the disposal.

3 marks

- The property is owned by the scheme and therefore cannot be used by creditors who are claiming against the company. This could also be a disadvantage is the company wants to borrow from a lender as the property would not be available as security for a loan.

Total 10 marks

(c)   The retirement pension can be provided in one of two different ways.

1 mark

- Firstly, an annuity may be purchased to provide an income for life.

1 mark

- Alternatively, an income may be taken by withdrawal from the fund.

1 mark

- The amount drawn must be certified by an actuary.

2 marks

- The amount must be within 10% of the open market annuity available from the members fund.

1 mark
Total 6 marks

- The annuity purchase can only be delayed to age 75 at the latest.

(d)   When loans are made from the scheme to the principal employer there must be:

1 mark

- A genuine commercial purpose

1 mark

- A fixed term for the loan

3 marks

- A commercial rate of interest paid, 3% above bank base rate is specified unless it can be shown in writing that a similar loan could have been arranged elsewhere on better terms.

1 mark

- A written legal agreement

- Security for the loan unless it is for less than a year.

C4 (a) Pension would be £~~12,500~~. *[17500]*

£30,000 × 35/60 = £~~12,500~~ *[17500]*

(b) Maximum pension on retirement = £23,400

1 mark

Final remuneration = £30,000 + £2,100 + £1,500 = £33,600

2 marks

She is a post 89 member and will have completed 35 years service by Normal Retirement Date.

2 marks

As she has more than 20 years service, the Inland Revenue will allow her to take a 2/3 of final salary pension.

2 marks

Her existing provision must be taken into account.

1 mark

Additional pension of £23,400 – £~~12,500~~ *[17 500]* = £~~10,900~~ *[15900]* can be provided.

2 marks

Penny's maximum death in service lump sum would be 4 × £33,600 = £134,400.

2 marks

Her existing death in service benefits are £90,000.

1 mark

Therefore she can fund an FSAVC for an additional £44,400 in death benefits.

1 mark

In addition, Penny's personal contributions will be refunded.

1 mark

She could also fund to increase spouse's and dependants' pensions.

1 mark

Maximum pension for spouse would be 2/3 of Penny's pension at NRD

2 marks

2/3 × £23,400 = £15,600.

1 mark

Existing scheme pension for spouse is 50% × £~~12,500~~ *[17500]* = £~~6,250~~ *[8750]*.

2 marks

There is scope to provide for a further £15,600 – £~~6,250~~ *[8750]* = £~~9,350~~ *[6850]*.

2 marks

Maximum pension payable to dependants would be 1/3 × £23,400 = £7,800.

2 marks

Existing provision amounts to 20% × £~~12,500~~ *[17500]* = £~~2,500~~ *[3500]*.

2 marks

Therefore additional dependants' pensions of £7,800 – £~~2,500~~ *[3500]* = £~~5,300~~ *[4300]* could be provided by an FSAVC.

2 marks
Total 29 marks

(c) Guaranteed Minimum Pensions (GMP) ceased to accrue from 6 April 1997.

1 mark

GMP was replaced by a reference scheme/requisite benefit test.

2 marks

The scheme must provide a pension based on 90% of 'band' earnings.

1 mark

It must be paid from age 65.

1 mark

A spouse's pension of 50% of the members pension must be provided.

2 marks

Accrual rate must be at least 1/80th of 90% band earnings for each year of service and limited price indexation applies.

2 marks
Total 9 marks

C5 (a) A pension fund withdrawal/income drawdown plan would be ideal for Chris's needs, as this will allow him to take the tax-free cash from his fund and also take an income to supplement his consultancy earnings. As Chris is retiring early, if he purchased his annuity at the present time he is likely to get a poor annuity rate. If Chris delays the purchase of the annuity, it is hoped that as he gets older the annuity rate will improve, although this is by no means guaranteed.

5 marks

2 marks

2 marks

Total 9 marks

If Chris delays the purchase of the annuity it is hoped that as he gets older the annuity rate will improve, although this is by no means guaranteed.

Pension fund withdrawal means that Chris's fund can remain invested in equities and benefits from the higher potential growth fund than if he bought his Compulsory Purchase Annuity.

1 mark

(b) Chris is not contracted out of SERPS therefore there are no protected rights funds to take account of in the tax-free cash calculation.

1 mark

Chris may therefore take $25\% \times £568,000 = £142,000$

1 mark

This would leave a residual fund of £426,000.

1 mark

If the fund had been a retirement annuity plan, then the amount of tax-free cash that could be taken would be dependent on the prevailing annuity rate.

1 mark

Chris would not be able to benefit directly from a Retirement Annuity Plan as he is not yet aged 60.

1 mark

Retirement Annuity Plans can have a higher potential tax-free cash lump sum than a Personal Pension because the tax free cash is set at three times the residual pension.

2 marks

The annuity rate is based on a level annuity, which is paid annually in arrears, with no guaranteed period. This will give a high annuity rate.

2 marks

Total 10 marks

If the annuity rate is greater than 11.11%, a Retirement Annuity Plan will give greater tax-free cash than a Personal Pension and if less than 11.11% a Personal Pension will offer more tax-free cash.

2 marks

(c) The factor that would be used in the tables is £66. We round down to the nearest 0.25% in the tables and Chris is currently aged 52.

1 mark

£66 is the maximum annual income per £1,000 of fund.

1 mark

The fund value was £568,000 and maximum tax-free cash of £142,000 is to be taken, leaving a fund value of £426,000.

1 mark

This would mean that the maximum income that may be taken under the GAD limits is:

1 mark

$£66 \times 426 = £28,116$

1 mark

The minimum income that may be taken is 35% of the maximum income:

1 mark
Total 8 marks

35% of £28,116 is £9,840.60.

(d) There are a number of risks associated with the use of a draw-down plan to provide income.

1 mark

- The annuity purchase may be delayed only to age 75 and not indefinitely.

1 mark

- There is no guarantee that annuity rates will improve with age.

2 marks

- Due to the high level of charges of this scheme and the withdrawals from the fund it is necessary for the fund to remain in equities to reduce the chance of the fund becoming eroded.

1 mark

- Investments in equities carry a higher risk than say with-profits funds that would usually be selected close to retirement.

1 mark

- If the fund value does become depleted it may be necessary at the three yearly review to reduce the amount of income that is taken from the fund.

1 mark

- There is also 'mortality drag' to contend with.

1 mark

- This is a form of lost investment return.

- The reason is that any mortality subsidy is lost from those people who have died before their life expectancy has expired.

Marking scheme
1 mark

Total 9 marks

(e) In the event of Chris's death the options that are available to the surviving spouse or other dependants are as follows.

- Income withdrawal can continue until the surviving spouse or dependant reaches the earlier of age 75, or the date when the deceased member would have reached aged 75. *(2 marks)*

- The surviving spouse may purchase an annuity in the normal way. *(1 mark)*

- The remaining fund may be taken as a lump sum but liable to a tax charge of 35%. *(1 mark)*

Total 4 marks

C6 (a) Nigel had seven years service with Royal Bank of Caledonia. *(1 mark)*

His final pensionable salary was £60,000 *(1 mark)*

The scheme was based on 1/60th for each year of service. *(1 mark)*

$7 \times 1/60^{th} \times £60,000 = £7,000$ *(1 mark)*

Total 4 marks

(b) The revalued pension is £7,000 per annum and of this £750 per annum is GMP. *(1 mark)*

The GMP will revalue at 6.25% pa for 17 tax years to normal retirement age. (You are expected to know the GMP revaluation dates and rates. *(1 mark)*

The revaluation factor is therefore $1.0625^{17} = 2.8028$. *(1 mark)*

The revalued GMP is $£750 \times 2.8028 = £2102.10$ pa. *(1 mark)*

The excess over GMP at the date of leaving is £7,000 less £750 = £6,250 pa. *(1 mark)*

This is subject to statutory revaluation ie 5% pa for 17 years. *(1 mark)*

The revaluation factor is $1.05^{17} = 2.292$. *(1 mark)*

Therefore the revalued non-GMP component is $£6,250 \times 2.292 = £14,325$ pa. *(1 mark)*

The total revalued pension is therefore $£14,325 + £2,102.10 = £16,427.10$. *(1 mark)*

Total 9 marks

(c) The transfer value is worked out in four steps.

The first step is to calculate the preserved pension at the date of leaving. *(1 mark)*

The second step is to work out the revalued pension at the date of retirement. Here the split between GMP and non-GMP will be taken into consideration. *(2 marks)*

The third step involves calculating the cost of buying a revalued pension at normal retirement date. The capital cost of buying the revalued pension is calculated by dividing the revalued figure worked out in Step 2 by the appropriate annuity rate. *(1 mark)* *(1 mark)*

Annuity rates have to be assumed for each of the component (The GMP and the non-GMP component). The GMP component has to be subdivided between pre-April 1988 GMP and post-April 1988 GMP. This is because the pre-April 1988 is increased by RPI up to 3% and the scheme itself has no mandatory liability for escalating this element of the revalued GMP, as the DSS takes care of the revaluation. With regard to the post-April 1988 GMP the scheme must as a minimum provide for escalation at RPI to a maximum of 3% per annum with the DSS providing for any top up necessary to give full RPI escalation on this part of the benefit. Hence different annuity rates will be used to provide the different elements of the pension. *(1 mark)* *(1 mark)* *(1 mark)* *(1 mark)*

The fourth step involves discounting the figure worked out in Step 3 back to the present day using an assumed rate of growth for the fund. *(1 mark)* *(1 mark)*

BPP PUBLISHING

Marking scheme

1 mark

1 mark

1 mark

1 mark

Total 15 marks

Guidance is given in a document issued by the Institute and Faculty of Actuaries called GN11. Basically, GN11 requires that regard is given to the yield to redemption on gilts. Equally, following the Pensions Act, schemes will tend to have a consistency between the discount rate adopted for the purposes of calculating a transfer value (known as the cash equivalent), and that used for assessing the solvency position in relation to the minimum funding requirements laid down by the Act.

Often, the scheme actuary will take account of the investment mix of the scheme in determining the discount rate to be adopted but generally the longer the term to retirement the greater the emphasis there may well be on equity based rates of return.

(d)

Personal Pension	*Section 32 Buy-Out Bond*
The fund is available to purchase survivor's benefit. 1 mark	The total fund value may be used to provide survivor's benefits. 1 mark
Nigel's widow, if she is a qualifying spouse, will have to buy a pension with the protected rights fund. 2 marks	In the first instance the GMP for the spouse has to be purchased. 1 mark
The maximum lump sum tax-free cash is limited to 25% of the fund value. 1 mark	The death in service lump sum of up to four times the leaving salary may be paid but this is not revalued by RPI. 2 marks
The pension must escalate at 3% pa or 3% if less. 1 mark	Any remaining fund may be used to buy dependants' pensions. 1 mark
If there is no qualifying spouse on death then the protected rights fund may be paid out as cash. 2 marks	

C7   (a)   The reasons an employer may wish to establish a FURBS are as follows.

Where the employee is currently earning in excess of the earnings cap and is a post-89 member of the exempt approved occupational scheme. A FURBS will be the only method which will allow the employer to provide pension benefits in respect of earnings that exceed the earnings cap.

Inland Revenue rules allow a full 2/3rds pension to be taken after 20 years service for both 87-89 and post-89 members of the scheme. If the employee is unable to complete this amount of service the employer may wish to provide benefits that are in excess of the Inland Revenue maximum.

The maximum pension that may be provided by an approved scheme is 2/3rd of final remuneration in normal circumstances. Should the employer wish to provide benefits in excess of 2/3 of final remuneration, an unapproved scheme would be appropriate for the amount of the excess.

Maximum benefits limit the Death in Service pension to four times final remuneration plus reasonable interest and a return of member contributions. Should the employer wish to provide Death in Service benefits in excess of four times final remuneration an unapproved scheme would be appropriate.

Where the employee contributes to a personal pension plan, the employer may wish to fund for death benefits through an unapproved arrangement. This will enable the employee to make only contributions towards his/her retirement fund, rather than having to provide death benefits in addition.

Where the company is an investment company the only approved arrangement that directors can opt for is a Section 590 scheme, which has very restricted benefits. Should the employer wish to provide benefits in excess of those available under the Section 590 scheme then they may wish to establish an unapproved scheme to achieve this objective.

Where the firm wishes to use its pension fund to allow unrestricted self-invest then again an unapproved arrangement could be a viable option.

1 mark

The benefits of an unapproved arrangement for employees are as follows.

1 mark

Where the employee (who is a post-89 member of the approved scheme) is earning in excess of the earnings cap then it may be preferable for them to have an unapproved scheme to provide benefits for the excess.

1 mark

The unapproved arrangement is not restricted to providing maximum benefits after a certain number of years and therefore could be an attractive option for those employees who are unable to complete 20 years service.

1 mark

The benefits that can be provided by an unapproved scheme are virtually unrestricted.

1 mark

The employee may be attracted to the inheritance tax planning aspects of a FURBS given that there is generally no inheritance tax to pay on distributions from the fund on death.

1 mark

As the FURBS may provide death benefits, it is attractive for employees who have only a personal pension, as they will no longer have to pay life premiums. This money can be used to increase the value of their pension fund.

1 mark

For the reasons outlined above, directors of investment companies will wish to be a member of an unapproved arrangement to provide benefits in excess of those available under a Section 590 scheme.

1 mark

FURBS will provide a tax-free lump sum on retirement. However, if a pension is taken, this will be taxed.

1 mark

The fund may be taxed in a more beneficial way than the member.

1 mark
Total 16 marks

(b) (i) • A FURBS is a Funded Unapproved Retirement Benefit Scheme.

1 mark

    • An employer establishes a FURBS usually to provide benefits for senior employees who earn in excess of the earnings cap or are unable to complete enough service with the company to provide an attractive pension package.

2 marks

    • A fund is established under trust, and the assets of the fund are separate to those of the employer. Each member has an earmarked fund.

1 mark

    • The employee has to pay tax on the contributions made by the employer to the fund as these are treated as a benefit in kind.

1 mark

    • Employer contributions are fully deductible for tax purposes.

1 mark

    • The contributions are, however, subject to NICs.

1 mark

    • The investment income of the fund and any capital gains are subject to UK tax in the normal way.

1 mark

    • A FURBS is designed to provide a lump sum on retirement, which will be free of tax. Any pension paid would be taxable.

1 mark

    • Contributions are not normally made by the member into the fund because they do not benefit from tax relief.

1 mark

(ii) • UURBS is an Unfunded Unapproved Retirement Benefit Scheme.

1 mark

    • They are simply a promise from the employer to provide benefits on retirement, there is no funding of this arrangement.

1 mark

    • Under the Statements of Standard Accounting Practice 24 (SSAP 24), the employer must establish a book reserve in the accounts of the company.

1 mark

BPP
PUBLISHING

Marking scheme
1 mark

- There are no costs to the employer at the time of establishing the scheme, as it is not funded.

1 mark

- The company does not benefit from tax relief until the benefits are paid out to the member.

1 mark

- As contributions are not being made, there is no National Insurance liability.

1 mark

- The employee does not have to pay tax on the promise at the time it is made.

1 mark
Total 18 marks

- Pension benefits would be taxable on the employee at the time they are paid out.

(c) The options that are open to an individual who is a member of an unapproved scheme will depend upon whether the scheme is a FURBS or an UURBS.

The options available in respect of the FURBS are as follows.

1 mark

- As the member has more than two years service with the employer, it is possible to leave the FURBS fund with them.

1 mark

- In addition the employee could transfer the benefits to his new employer's FURBS, if they are willing to accept it.

1 mark

- The employee may decide to take the benefits early if they are aged over 50.

The options available in respect of the UURBS are as follows.

1 mark

- Leave the UURBS promise with the previous employer.

1 mark

- Transfer the benefits from the UURBS to the new employer. (This would mean the new employer receiving a transfer value, so the UURBS will become a FURBS and there will be a tax charge as a consequence).

1 mark
Total 6 marks

- Take benefits early.

C8 (a) He is aged 52 so the relevant percentage is 30%

2 marks

$30\% \times £70,000 = £21,000$

(b) The two main options available to a company director are to either contribute to a personal pension arrangement or for the employer company to establish an occupational pension scheme.

Total 2 marks

1 mark

The personal pension plan may be either a straightforward insured arrangement or could possibly be a Self-Invested Personal Pension.

1 mark

The occupational pension scheme could be either an Executive Pension Plan or a Small Self Administered Scheme.

Self Invested Personal Pensions and Personal Pensions

1 mark

John may pay a percentage of his net relevant earnings into the fund. The percentage is based on John's age at the start of the tax year.

2 marks

The pension at retirement is not limited by the Inland Revenue. It is only limited by the annuity rate, or other drawndown arrangement, and the size of the fund.

2 marks

The employer may also contribute to the pension fund, but this will be included in the overall amount that may be contributed. There will be a saving in national insurance contributions when the employer pays into the fund.

1 mark

Tax relief is available for both employer and employee contributions.

The SIPP fund may be used to purchase property.

1 mark

SSAS and EPP

The Inland Revenue allow the employee to take benefits equivalent to 1/60th of final remuneration for each year of service.

1 mark

It is possible to take benefits equivalent to 1/30th for each year of service but where this option is used it will be necessary to take into account retained benefits.

2 marks

It is not possible to contribute to the scheme in respect of the period before the firm was incorporated.

1 mark

Tax relief is available for both employer and employee contributions.

1 mark

If the fund is a SSAS, it may be used to purchase commercial property.

1 mark
Total 17 marks

(c) It would be appropriate to recommend a *SIPP* because the pension payable from this fund should be higher than the maximum possible from a SSAS.

2 marks

A SSAS would allow the John to take a pension of $10/60 \times £70,000 = £11,666$ (assuming salary remains constant).

1 mark

The SIPP, if maximum funded, would have a fund size as set out below.

Age	Contribution %	Salary	Contribution £
52	30	£70,000	21,000
53	30	£70,000	21,000
54	30	£70,000	21,000
55	30	£70,000	21,000
56	35	£70,000	24,500
57	35	£70,000	24,500
58	35	£70,000	24,500
59	35	£70,000	24,500
60	35	£70,000	24,500
61	40	£70,000	28,000
62	40	£70,000	28,000
		Total	262,500

3 marks

In addition there will be investment growth. Therefore a moderate annuity rate will lead to the pension being much higher than that available under SSAS.

2 marks
Total 8 marks

(d) *SIPP property purchase rules*

- The fund may not buy property from the member or anyone connected with the member, for example a spouse. The property may not be a residence, with an exception to cover a caretaker's flat, for example.

1 mark

- An independent valuation for the property must be undertaken.

1 mark

- A market rate of rent must be paid by the firm for renting the property.

1 mark

- It is possible for more than one SIPP to combine and purchase the property jointly.

1 mark

- From 6 April 2001, a SIPP borrowing for the purposes of property purchase or development, is restricted to a maximum loan of 75% of the purchase price or cost of development respectively. Any such loan must be secured on the property and must be repaid if the property is sold.

2 marks

SSAS property purchase rules

- The property may not be used as a residence, with limited exceptions. It must be commercial in nature.

1 mark

Marking scheme
1 mark

- An independent valuation of the property must be obtained.

1 mark

- The employer must pay a market rate of rent for the property.

1 mark

- The IR SPSS require notification of the purchase within 90 days.

2 marks

- There is a limit set on the amount of money that the SSAS may borrow. This is 3 times ordinary annual contributions plus 45% of the fund value.

1 mark
Total 13 marks

- It is possible to buy the property from the employer if they already own it.

Mock exams

G60 - Pensions

BPP Mock Examination 1

Question Paper:	
Time allowed	**3 hours**
You should answer all questions in Sections A and B, and two out of three questions in Section C. The paper carries a total of 200 marks, as follows:	

Section A	45 marks
Section B	75 marks
Section C	80 marks

You are advised to spend approximately 40 minutes on Section A, and 70 minutes each on Sections B and C. You are strongly advised to attempt ALL the required questions in order to gain maximum possible marks.

The numbers of marks allocated to each question part is given next to the question and you should spend your time in accordance with that allocation.

In attempting the questions, you may find it helpful in some places to make rough notes in pencil in the answer booklet. If you do this, you must cross through these notes before you hand in the booklet.

Tax tables are provided at the front of this Practice & Revision Kit.

Answer each question on a new page and leave several lines of blank after each question part.

It is important to show all steps in a calculation, even if you have used a calculator.

DO NOT OPEN THIS PAPER UNTIL YOU ARE READY TO START

UNDER EXAMINATION CONDITIONS

SECTION A
Answer all questions in this section

1   Joe, aged 65 has a retirement annuity fund of £100,000. Given an annuity rate for a single life pension payable annually in arrears with no guarantee of 9%, calculate the maximum tax free cash sum and reduced pension available from his retirement annuity plan.   **(6 marks)**

2   State and describe the changes to retirement benefits in the State Earnings Related Pension Scheme applicable for those reaching State Retirement age after 5 April 1999.   **(6 marks)**

3   (a)   Identify the circumstances in which benefits from a Freestanding AVC may be taken at a different time than the main pension scheme.   **(4 marks)**

    (b)   Describe briefly how the existence of a FSAVC may increase the tax free cash available from the main pension scheme.   **(4 marks)**

4   Outline the tax treatment of and limits applying to employer contributions to a Personal Pension Plan for the benefit of an employee.   **(6 marks)**

5   List the circumstances in which it is possible for an individual to be a member of both an Occupational Scheme and a Personal Pension arrangement.   **(7 marks)**

6   Identify the circumstances when it may be necessary for an occupational pension scheme to issue a 'lump sum certificate' when a transfer value is taken to a Personal Pension.   **(7 marks)**

7   (a)   Which schemes do the Transfer Club arrangements generally apply to?

    (3 marks)

    (b)   Explain briefly how the Transfer Club operates.   **(2 marks)**

SECTION B

Answer this question.

8   Gilbert Stewart, now aged 43, accepted voluntary redundancy terms from his previous employer in October 1995, when his salary was £68,000 pa and he then set up in business in his specialist field of hydrogeography offering services to the waste disposal industry.

Gilbert was a member of his previous employer's contracted-out final salary pension scheme giving a pension of 1/60th of final pay for each complete year of membership, with a 50% spouse's pension payable following death after retirement. The scheme anniversary is 1 May and has a normal retirement age of 65. This previous employer's scheme introduced the full requirements of limited price indexation on benefits accrued after 1 May 1992 in order to reduce scheme surplus, and at the time took a five year employer contribution holiday.

Gilbert joined service in November 1980, joining the pension scheme on the first scheme anniversary after a two year waiting period, the waiting period being excluded from the definition of pensionable service. He has the opportunity to take a transfer value of £125,300 into either a personal pension or a Section 32 buyout plan, of which £27,400 represents the GMP liability. A transfer analysis has revealed that a critical yield of 7.6% is required to match the benefits from the occupational scheme.

Gilbert's new business has grown dramatically as 2001 has progressed following the introduction of rigorous regulations on the requirements for new and existing landfill sites. Indeed Gilbert anticipates that his net relevant earnings for the 2001/02 tax year will be as much as £130,000, whereas over the previous tax year he only had net relevant earnings of £21,000.

Gilbert is keen to maximise his pension provision and intends to sell the business and retire when he is 50.

(a)   Calculate Gilbert's deferred pension benefits payable age 60 from the scheme of his previous employer. Ensure you show the specific levels of indexation to pensions in payment for each portion of the benefit.   **(17 marks)**

(b)   Explain and comment on the quoted critical yield, and how this and other factors might affect the decision of whether to take a transfer into a personal pension or a Section 32 plan.   **(19 marks)**

(c)   Gilbert wants to retire at the age of 50. Explain how this might impact on any decision to take a transfer value into either a personal pension or a Section 32 plan.   **(16 marks)**

(d)   Assuming that a transfer is taken into a personal pension and that Gilbert funds to the maximum possible over the period to age 50. Explain how he can ensure that his benefits are taken so as to match his overall income requirements.
          (15 marks)

(e)   What are the implications for the scheme of Gilbert's previous employer if the scheme surplus is not eliminated?   **(8 marks)**

          (Total: 75 marks)

SECTION C

Answer two of the following three questions.

9   George Cooper, who is single, joined British Filtronics, a large plc, as Finance Director in June 2001 at the age of 47, at a salary of £120,000 per annum. He has a retained pension from his previous employer's contracted in scheme of £17,850 per annum payable at age 60 which is subject to revaluation at 5% pa from his date of leaving service - May 2001.

George immediately joined the British Filtronics staff pension scheme which is contracted out and gives a benefit of 1/60th of final pay for each whole year of service payable at the age of 60.

In order to persuade George to accept the job, British Filtronics promised George that they would put arrangements in place to provide him with overall occupational pension benefits of 2/3rds of his final remuneration (excluding any benefits accrued from past employment), just as soon as they had been advised by their pensions consultants of how best to achieve this.

(a) (i) Calculate George's maximum pension and tax free cash benefits from the British Filtronics scheme at age 60 assuming that both his pay and the level of the earnings cap rise at 5% per annum between June 2001 and retirement. Show all of your workings.   **(17 marks)**

   (ii) Calculate the shortfall between what has been promised and the maximum pension benefit the scheme may provide.   **(7 marks)**

(b) (i) Identify the options open to British Filtronics to fill the gap between what has been promised and the maximum pension benefit the scheme may provide.   **(6 marks)**

   (ii) Explain the tax implications for the employee and the employer of the options open to British Filtronics to fill the gap between what has been promised and the maximum pension benefit the scheme may provide.

   (10 marks)

   (Total: 40 marks)

10   Patrick Jones died on the 3 June 2001 aged 48, leaving a widow aged 43 and two children aged 9 and 11.

Patrick was a member of a contracted in final salary occupational pension scheme with, in accordance with the scheme definitions, a final salary of £18,000 at the date of death. For some years prior to his death, Patrick had used an Appropriate Personal Pension for the purpose of contracting out of SERPs.

The occupational scheme of which Patrick was a member gives on death in service a lump sum death benefit of four times final pensionable earnings, based on the average of the last three earnings. Patrick joined the scheme on 1 June 1986 and paid in contributions to the scheme at the rate of 3% of pensionable pay.

In addition the scheme would have given at age 65 a pension of 1/80th of final pensionable salary in respect of each year of scheme membership. On death in service, the scheme gives a spouse's pension of 50% of the members accrued pension to the date of death.

(a) Explain and calculate the death benefit and pension that Patrick's widow will be entitled to from the occupational pension scheme.   **(7 marks)**

(b) What alternative definitions of final salary are allowed on death in service?

(7 marks)

(c) Describe the benefits that Patrick's widow be entitled to from his Appropriate Personal Pension. **(15 marks)**

(d) Calculate and explain the benefits that Patrick would have been entitled to in today's terms had he survived until normal retirement date. **(11 marks)**

(Total: 40 marks)

11   Tony Dunning is a provincial solicitor aged 53, who has recently returned to work after some 18 months away following a serious skiing accident, having made a full recovery.

Tony's has estimated net relevant earnings of £21,000 for tax year 2001/02, nil for tax year 2000/01 and £53,000 for tax year 1999/2000.

Tony has a number of existing pension policies. These comprise the following.

1   A With profits based Retirement Annuity set up in 1986 with Prudent Mutual with a premium of £100 per month originally, subsequent increases over the years have led to a contract with a current premium level of £160 per month. In the event of death before benefits are taken there will be a return of premiums with no interest. The policy will vest at age 70, and has a current transfer value of £32,450 with premiums paid to date of £14,700.

2   A Personal Pension set up in March 1989 with Moon Life with a monthly contribution of £100 on a return of fund basis. Tony thus far has invested into their managed fund. Tony nominated his first wife as the beneficiary on death in the event of death before benefits are taken.

Having married again two years ago, Tony is concerned that his wife should be catered for in the event of his death, but is also concerned about the cost of establishing further life cover.

Tony intends to retire before the age of 60 and intends to make substantial single pension contributions this year and in the future and so build towards a large fund at that time from which benefits will be taken.

(a) Identify and explain the options in relation to the Retirement Annuity contract in the light of Tony's concerns and objectives. **(14 marks)**

(b) Explain in detail the options open to Tony when he decides to take pension benefits. **(20 marks)**

(c) Explain how Tony may provide additional life cover for the benefit of his new wife. **(6 marks)**

(Total: 40 marks)

G60 - Pensions

BPP Mock Examination 2

Question Paper:	
Time allowed	3 hours

You should answer all questions in Sections A and B, and two out of three questions in Section C. The paper carries a total of 200 marks, as follows:

Section A	45 marks
Section B	75 marks
Section C	80 marks

You are advised to spend approximately 40 minutes on Section A, and 70 minutes each on Sections B and C. You are strongly advised to attempt ALL the required questions in order to gain maximum possible marks.

The numbers of marks allocated to each question part is given next to the question and you should spend your time in accordance with that allocation.

In attempting the questions, you may find it helpful in some places to make rough notes in pencil in the answer booklet. If you do this, you must cross through these notes before you hand in the booklet.

Tax tables are provided at the front of this Practice & Revision Kit.

Answer each question on a new page and leave several lines of blank after each question part.

It is important to show all steps in a calculation, even if you have used a calculator.

DO NOT OPEN THIS PAPER UNTIL YOU ARE READY TO START

UNDER EXAMINATION CONDITIONS

SECTION A

Answer all questions in this section.

1   Describe the main features of Funded Unapproved Retirement Benefits Scheme (FURBS). **(8 marks)**

2   Identify and explain the all the different circumstances in which taxation may arise on benefits paid from exempt approved occupational pension schemes.

(6 marks)

3   Following the implementation of the 1995 Pensions Act, describe the new arrangements for final salary schemes that contract out of the State Earnings Related Pension Scheme. **(7 marks)**

4   Identify the differences between in-house additional voluntary contribution schemes and free-standing additional voluntary contribution schemes. **(9 marks)**

5   Describe how limited price indexation (LPI) applies to occupational pension schemes and personal pension from 5 April 1997. **(7 marks)**

6   When an employee leaves a final salary Occupational Pension scheme that is contracted out, appropriate arrangements must be made for revaluing benefits to retirement age.

Explain briefly how these benefits will be revalued. **(8 marks)**

BPP PUBLISHING

SECTION B

Answer this question.

7   Carol Maunder, married and aged 52, has recently changed jobs. Carol's previous employer operated a contracted out final salary scheme of which Carol was a member until March 1997.

Carol has joined Gainsby Ltd who have recently introduced a Grouped Personal Pension Scheme open to any of their employee to join under written by Scottish Amiable and Gainsby Ltd are willing to match the contributions made by the employee to a maximum of 5% of salary.

Carol is concerned that she does the best thing in relation to the benefits from her previous employer's scheme and has asked you to advise her on what she should do.

(a) What options are open to Carol in relation to the benefits from her previous employer's scheme? **(12 marks)**

(b) Assume that Carol had more than two years membership of her previous employer's scheme.

Compile a list of the information you will need in order to be able to advise Carol:

(i)   From and in respect of the previous employer's scheme **(18 marks)**
(ii) From Carol **(13 marks)**

(c) Explain the risks associated with the decision to either leave the benefits where they are or to transfer them. **(22 marks)**

(d) Might a transfer to a personal pension in respect of Carol be subject to any form of certification? Explain your answer. **(10 marks)**

(Total: 75 marks)

SECTION C

Answer two questions from this section.

8   Norman Davis reaches his the normal retirement age under his employers Occupational Pension Scheme next month on his 60th birthday but intends to continue working for another three years.

He has over the last fifteen years been a member of his employer's n/60ths of final salary pension scheme although he joined service five years before he joined the scheme. Norman's final pensionable salary will be £90,000 and he is married to Janice who is fifteen years younger than Norman. They have two children aged twelve and fifteen.

(a) Calculate where possible and explain Norman's maximum allowable benefits from the scheme at normal retirement age.   **(20 marks)**

(b) State and explain the options are open to Norman as he is working on beyond the scheme's normal retirement age.   **(20 marks)**

(Total: 40 marks)

9   The four founding and controlling directors of Gamma Ltd, established twelve years ago, each earned £120,000, plus a £70,000 dividend last year.

The Directors want to make as much pension provision as they can.

Explain the advantages and disadvantages of:

(a) a Funded Unapproved Retirement Benefit Scheme (FURBS)   **(20 marks)**
(b) Executive Pension Plans (EPPs)   **(20 marks)**

(Total: 40 marks)

10 Albert Jones is 47 years of age and terminally ill, indeed he has been told that he can only expect to live for a maximum of nine months. Until he became unable to work just over a year ago, he worked for Petfood Supplies Ltd and was a member of their contributory and contracted in money purchase scheme with a pensionable salary of £18,000. Albert has been claiming benefit under his employers PHI scheme.

Albert has been contracted out of SERPs since the 1988/9 tax year through an appropriate personal pension but was a member of SERPs from April 1978 until he became contracted out.

Albert's wife does not work and is aged 42, and they have two children aged 13 and 8.

(a) Explain what options may be available in respect of Albert's benefits from the pension scheme.   **(17 marks)**

(b) Explain what options apply to the accumulated fund within the appropriate personal pension:

(i)   Immediately   **(2 marks)**
(ii) Following Albert's death   **(11 marks)**

(c) Explain the benefits that Albert's wife will be entitled to from the state following Albert's death.   **(10 marks)**

(Total: 40 marks)

BPP PUBLISHING

MOCK EXAM 1: ANSWERS

**DO NOT TURN THIS PAGE UNTIL YOU
HAVE COMPLETED THE MOCK EXAM**

WARNING! APPLYING THE MARKING GUIDES

If you decide to mark your paper using the marking schemes (reproduced at the end of each relevant BPP answer), you should bear in mind the following points.

1   The BPP answers are not definitive: we have applied our own interpretation of the marking scheme to our solutions to show how good answers should gain marks, but there may be more than one way to answer the question. You must try to judge fairly whether different points made in your answers are correct and relevant and therefore worth marks according to the marking scheme.

2   In numerical answers, do not penalise yourself too much for minor arithmetical errors: if you have followed the correct principles you should gain most of the marks. This emphasises the importance of including workings, which show the marker which principles you were following.

3   If you have a friend or colleague who is studying or has studied this paper, you might ask him or her to mark your paper for you, thus gaining a more objective assessment. Remember you and your friend are not trained or objective markers, so try to avoid complacency or pessimism if you appear to have done very well or very badly.

It is most important that you analyse your answers in detail and that you attempt to be as objective as possible.

SECTION A

1   Pension before cash = £9,000   1 mark

Reduced pension = £9,000 divided by 1.27 (1) = £7,086.61 (1)   2 marks

Tax free cash sum = 3 times reduced pension   1 mark

Therefore tax free cash sum is 3 × £7,086.61 (1) = £21,259.83 (1)   2 marks

2   SERPS will no longer be based on the best twenty years of average revalued band earnings.

SERPS instead will be based upon revalued life-time band earnings.   1 marks
                                                                                                            1 mark

Maximum SERPS will reduce in 0.5% stages to become a maximum   1 mark

of 20% of revalued life-time revalued band earnings for those retiring from 2009/10   2 mark
onwards.

Transitional relief applies to those who accrued SERPs between 1978 and 1988.   1 mark

3   (a) On leaving pensionable service, when the link with the occupational scheme is broken.

As long as the FSAVC is not 'linked' to a new employer's scheme by virtue of further   1 mark
contributions (in which case the FSAVC will be linked to the NRD of the new
employer's scheme).   2 marks

The employee may take benefit from the FSAVC between age 50 and 75 whether or not
they have actually retired.   1 mark

(b) The maximum tax free cash from the main scheme for a post-1989 regime member is
calculated as 2.25 × initial pension.   2 marks

The 'initial' pension will include the income from the FSAVC (1) and the main Scheme
(1).   2 marks

4   The overall maximum is based on age-related percentages of Net Relevant Earnings in the
current year,   1 mark

Or £3,600 pa gross if greater.   1 mark

Contributions by the employer reduce the maximum contribution the employee can pay.   1 mark

There is no carry back facility for employer contributions.   1 mark

The contribution is a deductible business expense.   1 mark

Employees are not taxed on the contribution and are not subject to National Insurance on   1 mark
it.

BPP
PUBLISHING

| Marking scheme | 5 | Where the Occupational Scheme gives Death in Service benefits only. |

<table>
<tr><td>1 mark
1 mark</td><td></td><td>Where the Occupational Pension Scheme is contracted in and an APP is used for the sole purpose of receiving State Scheme rebates.</td></tr>
</table>

½ mark — Where the Personal Pension only receives a transfer payment from another approved source.

½ mark — Where the individual has an additional source of non-pensionable income.

1 mark — Where the occupational scheme is a FURBS then the income remains non-pensionable income.

3 marks — £3,600 gross pa can be contributed by an occupational scheme member to a personal pension, where the individual has earned not more than £30,000 in at least one tax year in the five years preceding that in which the contribution is made, and is not a controlling director in the tax year of making the contribution nor at any time in the previous five tax years. In each case, years before 2000/01 are ignored. These are called the concurrency rules.

2 marks   6   Where the transfer is in respect of a member who at in any time in the previous ten years was a 20% director.

2 marks — Where the transfer is in respect of a person who in the previous ten years has earnings in excess of the earnings cap.

1 mark — Where the transfer is in respect of a member age 45 or over.

2 marks — Where the transfer is from an occupational pension scheme where the normal retirement age is 45 or less.

1 mark   7   (a)   Principal Civil Service Pension Scheme - Inner Club

1 mark — Public Sector Superannuation Schemes - Inner Club

1 mark — Some large private sector schemes mainly former public utility companies - Outer Club

(b) Employees who move from one employer in the Transfer Club to another are entitled to beneficial transfer terms (1) in the sense that any service under the previous employer could count in full for benefits under the new employer's scheme. (1)

2 marks

SECTION B

8   (a) Gilbert joined the scheme on 1 May 1983.   1 mark

On leaving he had 12 complete years of membership.   1 mark

So his deferred pension was 12/60ths of £68,000 ie £13,600 pa.   2 marks

The excess over the GMP (1) will be increased at 5% pa or RPI if less until age 60 (1).   2 marks

LPI applies for benefits over the GMP in respect of the post May 1992 period.   2 marks

This element of the deferred pension will not only be increased at 5% pa or RPI if less until age 60. (2) but will similarly increase in payment (1), as will the associated spouses pension. (1)   4 marks

The GMP could be revalued in accordance with Section 21 orders (1) giving full earnings indexation (1) or   2 marks

Will be based on fixed rate revaluation rate of 7% pa or   1 mark

Will be based on limited rate revaluation rate of 5% pa (1) with the payment of a limited revaluation premium to the DSS. (1)   2 marks

(b) The critical yield is the growth required for the transfer value to match the scheme benefits (1) at the scheme retirement date. (1)   2 marks

Achievement of a higher yield than 7.6% in either plan will give greater benefits based on the assumptions made in the analysis.   2 marks

Achievement of a lower yield than 7.6% in either plan will give lower benefits based on the assumptions made in the analysis.   2 marks

The critical yield appears to be low and may therefore favour the taking of a transfer value.   2 marks

The past performance in recent years of with profits and managed funds has generally given a return of more than 7.6% pa.   2 marks

However the preserved benefits in the previous employer's scheme are guaranteed (1) and the scheme is currently in surplus (1)   2 marks

There may therefore be further benefit improvements which may impact on deferred pensioners.   1 mark

This might improve Gilbert's deferred benefits.   1 mark

This might in the future improve the transfer value further.   1 mark

If the transfer is taken into a Section 32 plan, the guarantees under the GMP remains.   2 marks

If the transfer is into a personal pension the GMP converts into protected rights.   1 mark

Either way there is no guarantee that the scheme benefits will be exceeded.   1 mark

(c) Taking the preserved pension will need the trustees' consent if benefits are required earlier than age 60.   2 marks

The scheme benefits may be substantially reduced to take account of being taken early.   2 marks

The effect of this should be quantified.   1 mark

To take benefits early from the main scheme, an amount equal to the GMP will need to be payable by State Pension Age as a minimum.   2 marks

The critical yield may then be recalculated to the intended date at which benefits will be taken.   2 marks

BPP PUBLISHING

Marking scheme

This will determine whether it remains the case that the transfer represents good value for money.

1 mark

2 marks

If the trustees of the scheme do not generally allow benefits to taken early then Gilbert may wish to take the transfer value anyway.

1 mark

If the transfer is taken into a Section 32 plan, it will still be necessary for the GMP amount to be payable by State Pension Age.

1 mark

The GMP is however a small part of the overall benefits.

1 mark

If the transfer is taken into a personal pension, then the GMP converts into protected rights and the issue of having to cover the GMP disappears.

1 mark

However the protected rights element may only be taken from age 60 or later.

1 mark

(d) Gilbert may wish to use a phased retirement facility.

2 marks

By having the personal pension split into a large number of segments, he can vest as many segments as he wishes each year to meet his overall income requirements.

3 marks

Income will be represented by tax free cash from the vested segments (1) and the income arising from the segments being cashed in (1) as well as the cumulative income from the annuity arising from the earlier vesting of segments (1)

2 marks

Annuity must be purchased from any uncashed segments by the age of 75 at the latest.

1 mark

Alternatively or in addition Gilbert could use the income drawdown facility.

1 mark

Any tax free cash has to be taken at outset.

2 marks

Income is drawn from remaining fund at up to that calculated by reference to tables issued by the Government Actuary.

1 mark

Minimum permitted income withdrawal is at 35% of this maximum figure.

1 mark

Gilbert may vary income each year within these limits and so meet his income requirements.

1 mark

Undrawn fund must be used to purchased an annuity by the age of 75.

1 mark

(e) The scheme surplus if not reduced below 105% of the scheme liabilities

2 marks

Lack of action will result in that part of the fund in excess of this level (1) losing its tax free status.

2 marks

The surplus may be refunded to the employer if the IR SPSS approves.

1 mark

Any surplus so refunded will be taxed at the rate of 40%.

1 mark

This is a stand alone tax and is not affected the companies overall tax position.

1 mark

It may be possible to further improve benefits, reducing the surplus and so avoiding the taxation implications.

SECTION C

9   (a) (i)   This needs to be marked so that if a calculation error is made marks are given for the correct procedure.

Maximum benefits available from the scheme are as follows.

Pension

George's earnings for contributions purposes are capped at £95,400   1 mark

£95,400 indexed by 5% for 13 years = £179,891   2 marks

The maximum benefits allowable are the **lesser** of: 1 mark

(2/3rds × £179,891) minus retained benefits and   1 mark

(13/30ths × £179,891)   1 mark

Retained benefit of £17,850 will need to be revalued by 5% for 13 years = £33,659   2 marks

So the maximum pension is the lesser of:

£119,927 – £33,659 = £86,268   1 mark

and

£77,953   1 mark

However, he may be entitled to 'Normal Accrual' if higher   1 mark

Normal Accrual for him = 13/60ths × £179,891 = £38,976   1 mark

So the maximum pension he can take from the Scheme will be £77,953.   1 mark

The maximum tax free cash is expressed as 2.25 × initial pension.   1 mark

In this case the initial pension is the maximum pension of £77,953.   1 mark

Maximum cash = 2.25 × £77,953 = £175,394.   2 marks

Accept figures +/- £5 to allow for rounding

(ii)   Amount promised is 2/3rds of final revalued pay.   1 mark

Final pay will be revalued from today's figure of £120,000.

£120,000 becomes £226,227.   1 mark

2/3rds × £226,227 = £150,852.   2 marks

Scheme can give £77,953.   1 mark

Shortfall is £150,852 less £77,953 = £72,899.   2 marks

(b) (i)   Options to fill the gap are:

Enhance to maximum benefits under occupational scheme   1 mark

Executive Pension Plan topping up benefits under occupational scheme to maximum benefits   1 mark

Funded Unapproved Retirement Benefit Scheme (FURBS)   1 mark

Unfunded Unapproved Retirement Benefit Scheme (UURBS)   1 mark

Both FURBS and UURBS   1 mark

FURBS and UURBS plus maximum approvable benefits   1 mark

(ii)   *Tax implications*

Topping up approved options:

Marking scheme

1 mark Employer contributions are relievable as a trading expense.

1 mark Employer contributions are not chargeable to George as a benefit in kind.

FURBS

1 mark NICs payable on contribution by employer and if applicable employee.

1 mark Employer contributions will be assessable to the employee as a benefit in kind.

1 mark Thus will be taxed at the rate of 40%.

1 mark Account needs to be taken of the tax to be paid on the additional amount if George is to be no worse off.

1 mark Employer contributions receive tax relief.

1 mark To the extent that the contributions have been treated as a benefit in kind for the purposes of income tax.

1 mark To obtain relief the assets of the scheme should not be accessible to the company thus subject to a trust.

UURBS

1 mark There are no contributions so there are no tax implications for either party.

1 mark | 10 | (a) | Patrick's widow will be entitled to a lump sum of 4 × £18,000, = £72,000.

1 mark This will be paid at the discretion of the scheme trustees, so will not be an automatic entitlement.

1 mark The benefit will not form a part of Patrick's estate.

1 mark There will also be a return of Patrick's scheme contributions

1 mark and possibly these will be returned with interest.

Patrick's widow will also receive a widow's pension of

2 marks Half of 14/80th of £80,000 (1) ie £3,150 per annum (1) = £1,575.
[handwritten above £80,000: 18 000]

1 mark (b) Where there are no fluctuating emoluments, the annual rate of basic salary or wages being received immediately before death.

2 marks Basic salary or wages as above, together with the average of any fluctuating emoluments during the three years (or the whole period of employment if less) up to the date of death.

2 marks Total earnings (fixed plus fluctuating), paid during any period of twelve months ending not earlier than 36 months before the date of death.

2 marks Any earnings or fluctuating emoluments relating to other than the twelve months prior to the date of death may be increased in line with the Retail Prices Index to the date of death.

1 mark (c) Patrick's widow is a qualifying spouse.

Because although she is under the age of 45, she has two children in respect of which she will be receiving child benefit.

2 marks So Patrick's protected rights fund from his APP (1) will be used to provide for a spouse's pension. (1)

2 marks This pension will be purchased at rates which will include indexation at RPI or 3% if less (1) but the post April 1997 element must be indexed at RPI or 5% pa if less. (1)

The pension must be paid to the qualifying spouse at least until she either:

1 mark

(a) Dies, or

1 mark

(b) Remarries before state pension age

1 mark

The provider's rules may provide for the protected rights pension to be paid throughout the lifetime of the qualifying spouse.

1 mark

The spouse's pension may be guaranteed for a period of up to five years from its commencement date.

2 marks

Any further continuation of pension benefits following the death of the qualifying spouse may however only be for the benefit of any children for whom the spouse immediately before death was entitled to child benefit and only so long as at least one child is under the age of 18.

3 marks

Where the total value of the protected rights spouse's pension is under £260 per annum it may be commuted for cash.

1 mark

(d) At age 65, Patrick would have been entitled to a pension of 31/80ths of his final pay.

1 mark

Based on his final pay at the date of death this would be £6,975 pa.

1 mark

Part of this could have been commuted for a tax free cash sum (1) of up to 93/80ths of final pay as a basic entitlement. (1)

2 marks

This could be augmented to up to 1.5 times final pay, £27,000 based on his final pay at the date of death if the scheme allows.

2 marks

Part of the pension could have been exchanged for a widow's pension.

1 mark

That part of the pension accrued after 6 April 1997 would have been subject to Limited Price Indexation.

2 marks

And so would have increased in payment at the lesser of 5% pa or the Retail Prices Index.

1 mark

The pension may have been guaranteed for up to 10 years.

1 mark

11. (a) Tony's retirement annuity policy can only provide a pension from age 60 at the earliest.

2 marks

In addition, the position on death is only a return of premiums.

1 mark

However the size of the transfer value given the premiums paid implies that the policy is performing well.

1 mark

A transfer to a personal pension would give a return of fund basis on death before retirement.

1 mark

A transfer could be made into a personal pension plan with Prudent Mutual that might have more favourable terms than transferring to another provider.

2 marks

A transfer could be made into the Moon Life personal pension into the managed fund (1) or into another available fund if a better fit to Tony's risk profile. (1)

2 marks

A transfer could be made into a personal pension with another provider.

1 mark

Following transfer benefits could be taken at any time before age 75.

1 mark

The tax free cash sum could be more or less than it would have been under the retirement annuity.

2 marks

This would depend on the annuity rates available at the time benefits were taken.

1 mark

(b) On retirement, Tony may take any cash sum and buy a pension on the open market.

2 marks

This may include provision for a spouse's pension and indexation.

2 marks

BPP
PUBLIS

Marking scheme

1 mark   Alternatively Tony could consider using staggered vesting.

1 mark   Here the arrangements are transferred into a plan with many segments.

2 marks   Tax free cash and pension bought each year in combination provide for the required income level.

1 mark   Any uncashed segments must be used to buy benefits by the age of 75.

1 mark   On death before the annuity is purchased, Tony's widow could take the remaining fund in cash.

1 mark   Another option would be to use income withdrawal.

1 mark   Here any tax free cash must be taken at the outset.

1 mark   The remainder of the fund stays invested and income is drawn from the fund.

1 mark   The income must not exceed the maximum allowed in accordance with the Government Actuary Department's tables

1 mark   and may not be less than 35% of that figure.

1 mark   Any undrawn fund must be used to buy benefits by the age of 75.

3 marks   On death before annuity is purchased Tony's widow could continue drawing down (1) purchase an annuity (1) or take the remaining fund in cash. (1)

1 mark   If taken in cash there would be a 35% tax charge.

(c)   Additional life cover can be provided for Tony's new wife by:

2 marks   Ensuring that the retirement annuity is changed to a return of fund basis either within the same plan (1) or by transferring to a personal pension. (1)

1 mark   Tony should consider changing the nominated beneficiary under the existing personal pension plan.

2 marks   Additional life cover could be purchased using personal pension term assurance.

1 mark   For plans such as this one that were set up before 6 April 2001, up to 5% of net relevant earnings could be used for this purpose.

MOCK EXAM 2: ANSWERS

DO NOT TURN THIS PAGE UNTIL YOU
HAVE COMPLETED THE MOCK EXAM

WARNING! APPLYING THE MARKING GUIDES

If you decide to mark your paper using the marking schemes (reproduced at the end of each relevant BPP answer), you should bear in mind the following points.

1   The BPP answers are not definitive: we have applied our own interpretation of the marking scheme to our solutions to show how good answers should gain marks, but there may be more than one way to answer the question. You must try to judge fairly whether different points made in your answers are correct and relevant and therefore worth marks according to the marking scheme.

2   In numerical answers, do not penalise yourself too much for minor arithmetical errors: if you have followed the correct principles you should gain most of the marks. This emphasises the importance of including workings, which show the marker which principles you were following.

3   If you have a friend or colleague who is studying or has studied this paper, you might ask him or her to mark your paper for you, thus gaining a more objective assessment. Remember you and your friend are not trained or objective markers, so try to avoid complacency or pessimism if you appear to have done very well or very badly.

It is most important that you analyse your answers in detail and that you attempt to be as objective as possible.

SECTION A

1   There is no income tax relief on employee contributions.

1 mark

Employer contributions are treated as a benefit in kind for income tax purposes. NICs are payable on employer and employee contributions (if earning are under the upper limit).

1 mark

Lump sum payments at retirement are free of tax but pensions are subject to income tax.

1 mark

Investment income is taxed at basic rate.

1 mark

Capital gains are subject to taxation but some relief is available so long as the scheme is set up under trust.

1 mark

Lump sum death benefits are outside of inheritance tax if paid through discretionary trusts.

1 mark

No contribution and no benefit limits.

1 mark

No investment restriction other than those consistent with prudent investments under trust law.

1 mark

2   Tax on refund to members at rate of 20%, after CEP where scheme contracted out. (CEP = Contribution Equivalent Premium)

2 marks

Income tax is payable on pensions to members and their dependants.

1 mark

Income tax is payable on commutation of trivial benefits for cash in excess of tax free limits.

1 mark

Income Tax arises on any excess over usual tax free limits where pensions are commuted for tax free cash in the event of serious ill-health.

1 mark

Tax will arise on any surplus AVCs arising that are refunded to the member at 32%/47.692%.

1 mark

3   From April 1997, contracted out final salary schemes have to meet a pension benefit bench mark in accordance with a statutory standard.

1 mark

GMPs no longer accrue from April 1997.

1 mark

The total of employer and employee National Insurance Contribution reduction in respect of the membership will be 4.6%.

2 marks

The pension benefit benchmark test will be based on an 80ths scheme (1) on 90% of band earnings with a 50% spouses pension (1) and subject to Limited Price Indexation. (1)

3 marks

4   Controlling directors may not have an FSAVC but may participate in an in-house AVC scheme.

1 mark

Headroom check for contributions £2,400 per annum or above applicable to FSAVC.

1 mark

Any limitation on contributions to in-house AVC will be as determined by the scheme actuary.

1 mark

Tax relief on FSAVC contributions at basic rate is available at source, with higher rate relief through annual assessment, with in-house AVCs contributions deducted from pre-tax earnings. Thus full relief is available at marginal rates.

1 mark

Investment choice much wider generally with FSAVCs than an in-scheme AVC.

1 mark

FSAVC contributions may continue if employment changes.

1 mark

May convert FSAVC to Personal Pension if no longer in pensionable employment.

1 mark

With in-house AVCs, payments must cease on changing jobs.

1 mark

Benefits arising from in-house AVCs may only be transferred if main scheme benefits also transferred.

5   LPI provides that pensions in payment must increase by the lower of 5% per annum and RPI.

Schemes may pay greater increases than this.

If more than LPI is paid one year, a lower increase is allowed the following year provided the two together at least match LPI.

Benefits affected are those accrued after 5 April 1997 in all occupational schemes.

Protected rights benefit applicable to personal pensions and rebate in respect of after 5 April 1997 are also subject to LPI.

Other personal pension benefits and all AVC/FSAVC benefits are exempt.

With regard to money purchase schemes, the member will receive less pension for his funds than on a level basis.

6   Revaluation of the pre April 1997 GMP may be in line with National Average Earnings.

This is in line of Section 21/Section 148 orders.

The GMP may be subject to fixed rate revaluation of 6.25% per annum.

The excess over the GMP for the period to 5 April 1997 is subject to revaluation at RPI or 5% if less.

Where fixed rate revaluation applies then any excess revaluation to full National Average Earnings indexation will be met by the State.

The post April 1997 benefit will be subject to revaluation at 5% or RPI or less.

SECTION B

7   (a) Retain benefits in her previous employer's scheme   1 mark

Transfer in to the new employer's GPP   1 mark

But GMP would convert to protected rights   1 mark

Retain the GMP in the employer's scheme if they will allow, whilst transferring the
excess to the GPP   1 mark

Transfer to another personal pension of Carol's choice   1 mark

Transfer the GMP (1) and excess (1) to a Section 32 Buyout plan   2 marks

Split the transfer between a Section 32 plan so as to provide the GMP and take the
balance to a personal pension scheme   1 mark

If she had less than two years membership, take a refund of her own contributions (1)
less tax at 20% and her share of the contributions equivalent premium (1)   2 marks

Take immediate early retirement benefits (1), as she is over age 50. (1)   2 marks

(b) (i)   The amount of the preserved benefits payable at normal retirement date (1) with
revaluation taken into account. (1)   2 marks

Scheme normal retirement date   1 mark

Early retirement benefits whether permitted (1) and any actuarial penalties (1)   2 marks

Structure of preserved benefits for example post retirement escalation of
benefits, guarantee periods.   2 marks

Have there been any discretionary benefit increases historically in relation to
pensions in payment (1) in particular in relation to those with deferred benefits?
(1)   2 marks

The amount of any tax free cash sum   1 mark

The amount of the GMP (1) and how it splits into the pre and post April 1988
periods (1)   2 marks

The amount of the transfer value available and how it splits as to the GMP (1)
and the excess over GMP(1)   2 marks

Is the scheme in surplus?   1 mark

Does the scheme participate in any transfer club arrangements?   1 mark

Have any discretionary increases in benefits been taken account of in the
transfer value?   1 mark

The amount of any death benefits   1 mark

(ii) Carol's attitude to investment risk   2 marks

Date of intended retirement (1) and whether earlier than the scheme NRD (1)   2 marks

Carol's Salary in her current (1) and her previous job (1)   2 marks

Final pensionable salary at the date of leaving her previous job   1 mark

How important is security of benefits?   1 mark

Does Carol have any dependants who could receive benefits?   2 marks

Is there any intention to change jobs again?   1 mark

Or to become self employed?   1 mark

1 mark

Carol's attitude towards her previous employer?

2 marks

(c) Retained benefits are guaranteed (1) but may vary depending on the revaluation basis. (1)

2 marks

If revaluation is at a fixed rate, then the preserved benefit is known in amount (1) whereas if it is subject in any way to retail price movement then this introduces some uncertainty. (1)

1 mark

Higher inflation would lead to the real value of the benefits falling.

1 mark

Both personal pension and Section 32 buyout plans are money purchase based.

2 marks

Benefits may therefore be higher or lower than the revalued preserved benefits.

3 marks

This will depend on investment performance (1), charges (1), and annuity rates (1) at the time benefits are taken.

2 marks

A Section 32 plan will give a guarantee however in relation to the GMP

2 marks

When the critical yield is calculated, it is based on certain assumptions as required by the PIA.

1 mark

If these assumptions are not met then this increases the risk of the scheme benefits not being at least matched.

1 mark

The term to retirement age is relatively short.

1 mark

The investment risk associated with a personal pension or section 32 transfer is more acceptable where the term is relatively long.

2 marks

If Carol should change jobs again, there could be a company scheme that it would be more beneficial to transfer to.

2 marks

This is particularly so if the scheme of any later employer offered added years (1) or if the previous and any new employer were members of a transfer club. (1)

2 marks

(d) Certification of the maximum tax free cash would be required:

1 mark
1 mark

As Carol is over age 45
or if she earned more than the earnings cap at any time in the last ten years.

1 mark
1 mark

Without such a certificate then no tax free cash could be paid
if she has been a controlling director in the last ten years.

2 marks

A general or overfunding certificate would be required:

1 mark
1 mark

If Carol earned more than the earnings cap at any time in the last ten years
or if she has been a controlling director in the last ten years.

SECTION C

8   (a) Maximum scheme pension benefits would be:

The greater of 20/60ths of final salary (1) and the earnings cap does not apply (1)   *2 marks*

ie £30,000   *1 mark*

or

2/3rds of final salary (1) as Norman is a pre 1987 member (1)   *2 marks*

ie £60,000 pa   *1 mark*

less any retained pension benefits   *1 mark*

guaranteed for up to ten years   *1 mark*

plus a widow's pension on death after retirement of up to 2/3rds of his own maximum pension   *1 mark*

ie £40, 000 pa   *1 mark*

plus additional children's pensions on death after retirement   *1 mark*

but the combination of the widow's pension and the children's pensions may not exceed his own pension.   *1 mark*

✳   These pensions may commence on Norman's death or at the end of any guaranteed period in relation to Norman's own pension   *1 mark*

Own and dependants' pensions may be increased in payment up to in line with RPI   *1 mark*

Maximum tax free cash will be the greater of 60/80ths of final salary   *1 mark*

ie £67,500   *1 mark*

or 1.5 times salary   *1 mark*

ie £135,000   *1 mark*

less any retained tax free cash benefits   *1 mark*

plus reduced pension benefits   *1 mark*

    (b) Norman may:

Take pension and tax free cash now or defer all benefits until later   *1 mark*

Take any tax free cash now and defer taking his pension until later   *1 mark*

If scale benefits apply then additional 60ths could be granted in respect of post NRD service giving a total of 23/60ths   *1 mark*

Additional tax free cash by way of commuting pension could be allowed at the rate of 3/80ths of final pay for each year of post NRD service   *1 mark*

making a total of 69/80ths of final pay   *1 mark*

Final pay may be calculated as at the date of actual retirement   *1 mark*

The benefits applicable at normal retirement age could be actuarially increased or RPI indexed   *1 mark*

If Norman decides to take all scheme benefits: he could be re entered in to the main scheme and earn up to 3/60ths of final pay as a further pension   *1 mark*

Part of this may be commuted for up to 9/80ths of final pay as tax free cash   *1 mark*

There will be no retained benefit issues   *1 mark*

But as a post 1989 member he would be subject to the earnings cap   *1 mark*

Marking scheme			The same outcome could be achieved from an EPP
1 mark 1 mark			If Norman's employer was unwilling to contribute then salary sacrifice would be an option to achieve the same outcome.
1 mark			Or Norman could take out a personal pension as he will now be in non-pensionable employment and his ongoing salary will count as net relevant earnings
1 mark			Norman's pension benefits will not count as net relevant earnings for this purpose
1 mark			But his ongoing pension and/ or part of his tax free cash may help 'fund' personal pension contributions
1 mark			Tax relief at 40% would be applicable on such contributions.
1 mark			Norman's employer could pay in to a personal pension for Norman
2 marks			Up to 35% of net relevant earnings could be paid in total, 40% from next tax year

9   (a)   *FURBS - Advantages*

1 mark	Allow almost unlimited investment flexibility
2 marks	So could invest in company shares and dividends would be subject to a lower rate of tax (23%) than the personal tax rates of the directors
2 marks	Favourable tax treatment on capital gains (1) as compared to personal taxation (1)
1 mark	So may be beneficial in relation to ownership of company shares.
2 marks	Employer contributions (1) and employee contributions (1) are unlimited
1 mark	Employer contributions are allowable against corporation tax
1 mark	Benefits are unlimited
2 marks	Directors can take account of all income sources including dividends in determining benefits
1 mark	The whole fund may be paid as a tax free cash sum
1 mark	Unlimited death benefits are available
1 mark	These may be set up under discretionary trust and so free of inheritance tax
1 mark	Can supplement approved occupational scheme arrangements which may also be set up

FURBS - Disadvantages

	Contributions from the employer are treated as benefit in kind
1 mark	No tax relief allowed on employee contributions
1 mark	Fund does not enjoy tax free income
1 mark	Fund does not enjoy tax free capital gains
1 mark	NICs on employer and employee contributions (if applicable)

(b)   *EPP - Advantages*

1 mark	The directors past service can be pensioned
1 mark	Loanbacks may be available if required
1 mark	May be easily 'converted' to a SSAS later if full investment facilities required
1 mark	Higher contributions will be allowed than to a Personal Pension despite new funding rules
1 mark	Contributions by the employer are not a benefit in kind
1 mark	And are not subject to National Insurance.

Employer contributions are allowable against Corporation Tax   1 mark

Employee contributions will get full income tax relief (1) at 40% (1)   2 marks

Pension fund grows free of tax on income and capital gains   1 mark

EPP may provide death in service lump sum   1 mark

This may be paid at trustees discretion and so free of Inheritance Tax   1 mark

EPP - Disadvantages

Maximum employer contributions are maximum benefit tested   1 mark

and subject to maximum funding rules as amended from June 1996   1 mark

Dividends may not be included in any pensionable salary definition   1 mark

Maximum employee contribution limited 15% of salary   1 mark

More administration and documentation than a personal pension plan   1 mark

Possible retained benefit problems in relation to any schemes of previous employers.   2 marks

Benefits are subject to the earnings cap.   1 mark

10   (a)   As Albert's life expectancy is less than 12 months   1 mark

The exceptional ill health provisions may apply   1 mark

He may be able to take the entire fund in the form of a cash sum   1 mark

However the trustees of the scheme will need to satisfy themselves as to Albert's medical condition   1 mark

Any part of that sum that exceeds the normal maximum cash entitlement will be subject to tax (1) at 20% (1)   2 marks

Albert may choose not to take any, part or all of the fund in this way   1 mark

Leaving the fund to provide benefits for his widow following his death   1 mark

This could be paid out at the discretion of the trustees to Albert's nominated beneficiaries and outside of his estate   2 marks

To a maximum of 4 times salary   1 mark

When added to any other separate death in service lump sum   1 mark

plus a return of his own contributions (1) with reasonable interest (1)   2 marks

The fund could be used to purchase a widow's pension of up to 4/9ths of Albert's final pensionable pay.   2 marks

Plus children's pensions   1 mark

(b)   (i)   Protected rights benefits may not be taken before age 60 even where the member is in serious ill health.   2 marks

(ii)   When Albert dies his widow will be a qualifying spouse   1 mark

As she is under age 45 but with one or more dependant children   2 marks

A spouse's annuity must be paid to the qualifying spouse at least until she either:
Dies   1 mark
or remarries before state pension age   1 mark
or whilst under the age of 45, ceases to reside with a child under the age of 16 or be entitled to child benefit in respect of a child under the age of 18.   1 mark

Marking scheme

1 mark

This is the minimum requirement to be contained in the personal pension rules. The personal pension may provide for the protected rights pension to be paid throughout the lifetime of the qualifying spouse in any event.

1 mark

The spouse's pension may be guaranteed for a period of up to five years from its commencement date.

1 mark

A continuation of pension benefits following the death of Albert's wife may apply so long as at least one child is still under the age of 18.

1 mark

The spouse's protected rights pension in payment must increase annually in line with retail prices index (1), to a maximum of 3% per annum. (1)

1 mark

If the total value of the protected rights spouse's pension is under £260 per annum then it may be fully commuted for cash.

2 marks

(c) Albert's wife will get a lump sum payment of £1,000.

1 mark

This is a tax free payment.

2 marks

She will be entitled to the widowed parent's allowance.

1 mark

This is a taxable benefit.

1 mark

It comprises an allowance for the widow and for each of the dependant children.

1 mark

This benefit ceases on remarriage.

2 marks

She will also inherit Albert's SERPS pension (the additional pension) applicable to the period when Albert was a member of SERPS.

ORDER FORM

BPP publish Study Texts and Practice & Revision Kits for papers of the Financial Planning Certificate and the Advanced Financial Planning Certificate. Each **Study Text** is tailored precisely to the syllabus. **Practice & Revision Kits** contain banks of questions and answers, plus full Mock Exams. **Success Tapes** are a new series of audio cassettes designed for revision on the move. You can order on our website or by telephone, fax or email.

We aim to deliver to all UK addresses inside 5 working days; a signature will be required. Orders to all EU addresses should be delivered within 6 working days. all other orders to overseas addresses should be delivered within 8 working days.

To: BPP Publishing Ltd, Aldine House, Aldine Place, London W12 8AW
Tel: 020 8740 2211   Fax: 020 8740 1184   Email: publishing@bpp.com   Website: www.bpp.com

Full name (Mr/Ms): _____

Daytime delivery address: _____

_____ Postcode: _____

Please send me the following:

	Study Text plus Kit	Qty	Study Text	Qty	Kit	Qty	Success Tape	Qty
Financial Planning Certificate (5/01)								
FP1: Financial Services and their Regulation	£44.95		£29.95		£19.95		£12.95	
FP2: Protection, Savings and Investment Products	£44.95		£29.95		£19.95		£12.95	
FP3: Identifying and Satisfying Client Needs	£44.95		£29.95		£19.95		£12.95	
Advanced Financial Planning Certificate (7/01)								
G10: Taxation and Trusts	£54.95		£39.95		£19.95		£12.95	
G20: Personal Investment Planning			£39.95					
G30: Business Financial Planning			£39.95					
G60: Pensions	£54.95		£39.95		£19.95		£12.95	
G70: Investment Portfolio Management			£39.95					
G80: Long-term Care, Life and Health Protection			£39.95					
H15: Supervision and Sales Management			£39.95					
H25: Holistic Financial Planning			£39.95					
K10: Retirement Options			£29.95					
K20: Pension Investment Options (12/01)			£29.95					

Subtotal ☐

Postage and packaging

UK: £3 for first Text, £2 for each extra   **p & p** ☐
    £2 for first Kit, £1 for each extra
    £1 for each Tape

Europe (inc ROI & CI): £5 for first Text, £4 for each extra
    £2.50 for first Kit, £1 for each extra
    £1 for each Tape

Rest of the world: £20 for first Text, £10 for each extra
    £15 for first Kit, £8 for each extra
    £4 for each Tape

Total ☐

I enclose a cheque for £_____ (Cheques to BPP Publishing Ltd) or charge to my **Access/Visa/Switch**

Card number ☐☐☐☐ ☐☐☐☐ ☐☐☐☐ ☐☐☐☐ ☐☐☐☐

Start date (Switch only) _____ **Expiry date** _____ **Issue no. (Switch only)**_____

Signature _____ **Daytime Tel. (for queries only)** _____

For Updates, visit our website: www.bpp.com/fpc

REVIEW FORM & FREE PRIZE DRAW

All original review forms from the entire BPP range, completed with genuine comments, will be entered into one of two draws on 31 January 2002 and 31 July 2002. The names on the first four forms picked out on each occasion will be sent a cheque for £50.

Name: _____   Address: _____

_____

Date: _____   _____

How have you used this Kit?
(Tick one box only)

☐ home study (book only)

☐ on a course: at _____

☐ with 'correspondence' package

☐ other _____

Why did you decide to purchase this Kit?
(Tick one box only)

☐ recommended by training department

☐ recommendation by friend/colleague

☐ recommendation by a lecturer at college

☐ saw advertising

☐ have used BPP material in the past

☐ other _____

During the past six months do you recall *(Tick as many boxes as are relevant)*

☐ seeing our advertisement in *Financial Adviser*

☐ seeing our advertisement in *Money Management*

☐ seeing our advertisement in *IFA Contact*

Which (if any) aspects of our advertising do you find useful?
(Tick as many boxes as are relevant)

☐ prices and publication dates of new editions

☐ checklist of contents

☐ facility to order books off-the-page

☐ none of the above

Your ratings, comments and suggestions would be appreciated on the following areas.

	Very useful	Useful	Not useful
Introductory section	☐	☐	☐
Main text	☐	☐	☐
Questions in chapters	☐	☐	☐
Chapter roundups	☐	☐	☐
Quizzes at ends of chapters	☐	☐	☐
Practice examination	☐	☐	☐
Structure and presentation	☐	☐	☐
Availability of Updates on website	☐	☐	☐

	Excellent	Good	Adequate	Poor
Overall opinion of this Study Text	☐	☐	☐	☐

Do you intend to continue using BPP Kits?   ☐ Yes   ☐ No

Please note any further comments, suggestions and apparent errors on the reverse of this page, or write by e-mail to rogerpeskett@bpp.com

Please return this form to: Roger Peskett, BPP Publishing Ltd, FREEPOST, London, W12 8BR

REVIEW FORM & FREE PRIZE DRAW (continued)

Please note any further comments, suggestions and apparent errors below.

FREE PRIZE DRAW RULES

1   Closing date for 31 January 2002 draw is 31 December 2001. Closing date for 31 July 2002 draw is 30 June 2002.

2   Restricted to entries with UK and Eire addresses only. BPP employees, their families and business associates are excluded.

3   No purchase necessary. Entry forms are available upon request from BPP Publishing. No more than one entry per title, per person. Draw restricted to persons aged 16 and over.

4   Winners will be notified by post and receive their cheques not later than 6 weeks after the relevant draw date.

5   The decision of the promoter in all matters is final and binding. No correspondence will be entered into.